OXFORD PHILOSOPHICAL MONOGRAPHS

Editorial Committee:

Michael Dummett, Anthony Kenny
D. H. Rice, Ralph C. S. Walker

THE KANTIAN SUBLIME

The Kantian Sublime

From Morality to Art

PAUL CROWTHER

CLARENDON PRESS · OXFORD

1989

Oxford University Press, Walton Street, Oxford OX2 6DP

Oxford New York Toronto
Delhi Bombay Calcutta Madras Karachi
Petaling Jaya Singapore Hong Kong Tokyo
Nairobi Dar es Salaam Cape Town
Melbourne Auckland
and associated companies in
Berlin Ibadan

Oxford is a trade mark of Oxford University Press

Published in the United States
by Oxford University Press, New York

British Library Cataloguing in Publication Data
Crowther, Paul
The Kantian sublime: from morality to art.
—(Oxford philosophical monographs)
1. Aesthetics. Theories of Kant, Immanuel,
1724–1804
I. Crowther, Paul
111'.85'0924
ISBN 0–19–824848–2

Library of Congress Cataloging in Publication Data
Crowther, Paul.
The Kantian sublime: from morality to art / Paul Crowther.
p. cm.—(Oxford philosophical monographs)
Includes index.
1. Kant, Immanuel, 1724–1304—Contributions in concept of the
Sublime. 2. Sublime, The—History. [1. Kant, Immanuel, 1724–1804.
Kritik der Urteilskraft.] I. Title. II. Series.
B2779.C76 1989 111'.85—dc19 89–3024
ISBN 0–19–824848–2

Set by Hope Services, Abingdon
Printed in Great Britain by
Courier International Ltd.
Tiptree, Essex

For Paul H. Hirst and Juliet Simpson
and in memory of my grandfather
Harry Marsden

ACKNOWLEDGEMENTS

This work is the result of a number of years teaching and reflection on Kant's *Critique of Judgement*. It was written during a period of leave of absence granted by the University of St Andrews. This period was spent in the Subfaculty of Philosophy at the University of Oxford. The resulting work is a somewhat revised and extended version of a thesis which was accepted for the degree of D.Phil.

Portions of Chapters 2 and 3 were originally presented as papers for Professor Strawson's Kant Seminar in Trinity Term 1984. My thanks are due, therefore, both to him and to the other participants for their critical comments. Most of Chapter 6 has appeared under the title 'The Aesthetic Domain: Locating the Sublime' in the *British Journal of Aesthetics*. It reappears here by kind permission of the editor.

Special thanks are owed to Patrick Gardiner for his stimulating supervision of my work, and to Professor Michael Podro and Alan Montefiore, who examined the thesis and whose useful comments have shaped the present text at many points. Over the years my thinking on general philosophical matters has benefited greatly from discussion with Professor Martin Kemp, Juliet Simpson, Peter Suchin, Anton Long, Dr Christina Lodder, Louise Durning, Dr Patrick Murray, Dr Terry Diffey, Professor Hugo Meynell, Professor R. F. Atkinson, and Professor Paul H. Hirst. Thanks are also due to Mrs Eileen Carvell for her exemplary endeavours in typing the manuscript.

P.C.

CONTENTS

ABBREVIATIONS

Groundwork

I. Kant, *Groundwork of the Metaphysic of Morals*, trans. H. Paton (Hutchinson: London, 1955).

Judgement

I. Kant, *The Critique of Judgement*, trans. J. C. Meredith (Oxford University Press: Oxford, 1973).

Observations

I. Kant, *Observations on the Feeling of the Beautiful and the Sublime*, trans. J. Goldthwait (University of California Press: Berkeley, 1960).

Practical Reason

I. Kant, *The Critique of Practical Reason*, trans. L. W. Beck (University of Chicago Press: Chicago, 1949).

Pure Reason

I. Kant, *The Critique of Pure Reason*, trans. N. Kemp-Smith (Macmillan: London, 1973).

Introduction

The 1970s and 1980s have witnessed a major renewal of interest in Kant's aesthetics. Paul Guyer, Donald Crawford, Francis Coleman, Eva Schaper, Theodore Uehling, Salim Kemal, and Mary McCloskey have all written books explicitly devoted to the topic;[1] Guyer and Ted Cohen have edited a collection of relevant essays;[2] and Antony Savile and Mary Mothersill have written widely praised general works which involve much discussion of Kant's aesthetic theory.[3] These approaches, however, have concentrated almost exclusively on Kant's treatment of beauty and art. His extensive discussion of the sublime, in contrast, has received scant attention. This neglect is a general characteristic of the reception of Kant's aesthetics in the Anglo-American and German traditions of philosophy in the twentieth century. The reasons behind it have been usefully summarized by Paul Guyer. He suggests that Kant's theory of the sublime does not fit in well with the general framework of *The Critique of Judgement*—and in particular with the account of aesthetic experience. Indeed, he goes so far as to say that

even if there is historical interest in Kant's discussion of the sublime, I think it is safe to assume that his analysis of this particular aesthetic merit will not be of much interest to modern sensibilities, and thus that

---

[1] Paul Guyer, *Kant and the Claims of Taste* (Harvard University Press: London and Cambridge, Mass., 1979; Donald Crawford, *Kant's Aesthetic Theory* (University of Wisconsin Press: Madison, 1974); Francis Coleman, *The Harmony of Reason: A Study in Kant's Aesthetics* (University of Pittsburgh Press: Pittsburgh 1974); Eva Schaper, *Studies in Kant's Aesthetics* (Edinburgh University Press: Edinburgh, 1979); Theodore Uehling, *The Notion of Form in Kant's Critique of Aesthetic Judgement* (Mouton & Co: The Hague, 1971); Salim Kemal, *Kant and Fine Art* (Clarendon Press: Oxford, 1986); Mary McCloskey, *Kant's Aesthetics* (Macmillan and Co: London, 1986).

[2] Ted Cohen and Paul Guyer (eds.) *Essays in Kant's Aesthetics*, (University of Chicago Press: Chicago, 1982).

[3] Antony Savile, *The Test of Time* (Clarendon Press: Oxford, 1981); Mary Mothersill, *Beauty Restored* (Clarendon Press: Oxford, 1984).

most of what we can or will learn from   must come from his
discussion of judgements of beauty.[4]

To these worries must be appended t   ier problems. First,
Kant's discussion of the sublime is   lably difficult; and
second, the term 'sublime' itself seems to be used so variably in
ordinary and critical discourse as to make any philosophical
definition of it seem unwarrantably stipulative.

In relation to this last objection, while the sublime is indeed
used very variably in ordinary and critical discourse, it seems to
operate nevertheless, within a broad twofold framework. On the
one hand, it is used *descriptively* to denote vast or powerful
objects and artefacts, or ones which induce extreme states of
emotion in us; on the other hand, it is used *evaluatively* in
relation to artworks of extraordinarily high quality. If we could
define the sublime in a way that could highlight important
connections between the two sets of usages, we would have a
definition with claim to more than merely stipulative validity. In
fact, it is a renewed confidence in the possibility of defining the
sublime which in part lies at the heart of an astonishing
transformation of sensibility which has taken place in the last ten
years or so. For while philosophers in the analytic tradition of
philosophy have found new significance in Kant's treatment of
beauty and art, philosophers from other traditions and, indeed,
writers in a host of other disciplines have asserted the cultural
centrality of the sublime—and, in particular, Kant's version of it.
Amongst the enormous literature here, one might cite the
following examples. Jacques Derrida and Paul de Man[5] have
offered extended (if difficult) analyses of Kant's theory of the
sublime; Neil Hertz[6] (amongst others) has related sublimity to
psychoanalysis; Thomas Weiskel and Louis Marvick[7] have

[4] Guyer, op. cit. (n. 1 above), 400.

[5] Jacques Derrida, *The Truth in Painting*, trans. G. Bennington (University of
Chicago Press: Chicago, 1987); Paul de Man, 'Phenomenality and Materiality in
Kant', in G. Schapiro and A. Sica (eds.), *Hermeneutics: Questions and Prospects*
(University of Massachusetts Press: Amherst, 1984).

[6] Neil Hertz, 'The Notion of Blockage in the Literature of the Sublime', in G.
Hartmann (ed.), *Psychoanalysis and the Question of the Text* (Johns Hopkins
University Press: Baltimore, 1978).

[7] Thomas Weiskel, *The Romantic Sublime: Studies in the Structure and
Psychology of Transcendence* (Johns Hopkins University Press: Baltimore, 1976);
Louis W. Marvick, *Mallarmé and the Sublime* (State University of New York Press:
Albany, 1986).

written books on Romanticism and Mallarmé's prose works (respectively) using Weiskel's reconstruction of Kant's theory as the core of their methodology; Jean-Francois Lyotard has published a number of extremely influential articles[8] which assign Kant's theory the most central role in defining modernism and postmodernism in art and culture generally. Whereas the concept of beauty seems outmoded—*passé* even—in relation to the current practices of criticism in the arts, sublimity has suddenly become—fashionable.

It is precisely this fashionable dimension of contemporary relevance which introduces a worrying aspect into these reappropriations of the sublime. Derrida and de Man's discussions, for example, examine Kant fundamentally in the context of recent poststructuralist approaches to language; Weiskel reconstructs Kant's theory on the basis of clues provided by structural linguistics and psychoanalysis; Lyotard uses Kant in a way that centres on sublimity's possible relevance to avant-garde modernist and postmodernist art. In all these cases, in other words, Kant's theory is put to use on the basis of, or in the service of, some much broader set of theoretical interests. There is little or no attempt to consider it in the context of possible tensions and distortions forced upon it by the broader philosophical position embodied in Kant's ethics and aesthetics. Until this issue is clarified, I would suggest that our understanding of both Kant and the status of sublimity as an aesthetic concept remain substantially incomplete. By addressing this issue, therefore, we will be able to both fill a gap in Kant scholarship and give more rigorous philosophical foundation to sublimity's contemporary relevance. The two aims of this study will be, accordingly, to trace the development and structure of Kant's theory of the sublime in the context of both his Critical ethics and aesthetics, and to derive from this a theoretically adequate account of the sublime as an aesthetic and artistic concept. My approach will be as follows.

In Part I of this study (Chapters 1 and 2) I shall first briefly outline the sublime as it is understood in sources available to Kant—notably the theories of Addison and Burke. I will then

---

[8] See esp. the essay included as an Appendix in his *The Postmodern Condition: A Report on Knowledge*, trans. G. Bennington and B. Massumi (Manchester University Press: Manchester, 1984).

trace how Kant adapts these approaches in his pre-Critical aesthetics, and how he goes beyond them by, in effect, stipulatively defining the sublime as a *moral* concept in his Critical ethics. In Part II (Chapters 3, 4, and 5) I will set the scene for a consideration of Kant's mature theory of the sublime, by first discussing how moral factors shape his overall strategy in the *Critique of Judgement* and also figure in his account of the judgement of taste. I shall then go on to elaborate and review Kant's structures and sources of argument in those sections of the third *Critique* that deal with judgements of sublimity. In particular, I will argue that, while his theory of sublimity does in fact fit in well with the overall strategy of the third *Critique*, the pressures of the Critical ethics are such that he does not succeed in establishing the aesthetic credentials of sublimity. In Part III (Chapters 6 and 7), however, by using some of Kant's basic insights, I will hope to establish these credentials and to apply the theory so derived to the work of art. I will then consider some of the more general implications of the theory.

Considering the wide ground to be covered by this study, and the necessary limitations on its length, it will not be possible to give Kant's concepts and arguments the kind of extensive and finely detailed analysis which has been provided, for example, by Paul Guyer. I will be concerned, rather, to provide working definitions of Kant's major concepts, and trace the broad development of his arguments. This means that (while pointing out the more important tensions and contradictions in Kant's position) I will try, wherever possible, to read him in terms of the interpretation which makes his arguments most plausible, rather than to consider various alternative (and perhaps equally viable) interpretations which would render his arguments implausible. There are, indeed, advantages to this more charitable approach, in so far as it enables us to retain a sense of the overall thrust and direction of his arguments, in a way that the more finely detailed approach might not.

I would finally point out that my reconstruction of a Kantian theory of the sublime in Part III will *not* attempt to offer any justification for those epistemological claims of universality and necessity which Kant makes for judgements of sublimity.

With these points in mind, I turn to Part I of my study.

PART I

Morality and the Sublime

I

The Background to Kant's Mature Theory of the Sublime

I

The sublime is an aesthetic concept of ancient lineage. In the eighteenth century, however, it underwent a major revival, and received especially important reformulations in the works of Joseph Addison and Edmund Burke. I shall now very briefly outline the salient aspects of these two theories in turn. First, through his conception of the 'great' (set out in his famous *Spectator* articles on 'The Pleasures of the Imagination') Addison is able clearly to separate those experiences which we would now commonly regard as 'sublime' from those which we would describe as 'beautiful'. He also gives an important description of what is positive in the experience of the sublime. Consider, for example, the following passage.

Our imagination loves to be filled by an object, or to grasp at anything that is too big for its capacity. We are flung into a pleasing astonishment at such unbounded views, and feel a delightful stillness and amazement in the soul at the apprehension of them. The mind of man naturally hates everything that looks like a restraint upon it, and is apt to fancy itself under a sort of confinement, when the sight is pent up in a narrow compass, and shortened on every side by the neighbourhood of walls or mountains. On the contrary, a spacious horizon is an image of liberty, where the eye has room to expatiate at large on the immensity of its views.[1]

On these terms, Addison's major claim is that our encounter with vast natural phenomena involves a sense of being liberated from perceptual confinement. We experience an exhilarating feeling of *self-transcendence*.

Edmund Burke's theory of the sublime, however, takes us in a

[1] Joseph Addison, *Collected Works* iii, ed. H. Bohn (Bell and Sons: London, 1890), 397–8.

somewhat different direction. In his *A Philosophical Inquiry into the Origins of Our Ideas of the Sublime and the Beautiful* (1757), his fundamental claim is that anything which can occasion pain or terror or some kindred passion is a potential source of the feeling of the sublime. This feeling can be occasioned in two different ways. First, when the perceptually overwhelming properties of objects test and strain our perceptual faculties so as to cause a weak state of pre-conscious pain; and second, where dangerous objects are encountered from a position of safety, thus causing a weak or moderated state of terror. In such cases as these, Burke informs us that

if the pain or terror are so modified as not to be actually noxious; if the pain is not carried to violence, and the terror is not conversant about the present destruction of the person, as these emotions clear the parts of a troublesome encumberance, they are capable of producing delight; not pleasure, but a sort of delightful horror; a sort of tranquility tinged with terror.[2]

For Burke, our delight in the sublime is due to the fact that the weak or moderated states of pain or terror which sublime objects arouse are ones which cause a healthy invigoration of those finer bodily tissues upon which the mental powers act. The feeling of the sublime is a feeling which is deeply bound up with our instinct for *self-preservation*.

With this background material in mind, we can now address Kant's early theory of the sublime.

II

Kant's first attempt to articulate a theory of the sublime is found in his pre-Critical *Observations on the Feeling of the Beautiful and the Sublime*, published in 1764. In the years immediately preceding this work, Kant had been much concerned with the relationship between feeling and morality, and Werkmeister is probably right in asserting that it was his indecision on this score which led him 'to take a closer look at the nature of feelings'.[3]

---

[2] Edmund Burke, *A Philosophical Inquiry into the Origin of Our Ideas of the Sublime and the Beautiful*, ed. John Boulton (Routledge & Kegan Paul: London, 1958), 136.
[3] W. H. Werkmeister, *Kant: The Architechtonic and Development of his Philosophy* (Open Court: London, 1980), 36.

Kant's method in the *Observations* is primarily descriptive and is conducted, as he puts it, 'more with the eye of an observer than of a philosopher'.[4] Nevertheless, the work does present some points of philosophical substance (especially in Chapter 1), and it is to an exposition of these that I now turn.

We are first informed that 'The various feelings of enjoyment or of displeasure rest not so much upon the nature of the external things that arouse them as upon each person's own disposition to be moved by these to pleasure and pain.'[5] It is this fact which explains why it is possible for one person to derive joy from, and another person to feel aversion towards, one and the same thing. Now it is important to note that while (in the above quotation) Kant uses the term 'feeling' to pick out particular instances of pleasure and displeasure, he subsequently—and much more frequently—uses it to denote the subjective *disposition* which enables us to find things pleasurable or displeasurable. Thus Kant considers (amongst others) the stout man who likes a coarse joke, the merchant who enjoys calculating his profits, and the man who finds the opposite sex a mere object of pleasure: 'all these have *a feeling that makes them capable* [my emphasis] of enjoying pleasures after their own fashion'.[6] Kant clearly regards this capacity for feeling as somewhat crude, inasmuch as it can be employed 'without any thought whatsoever'. There is, however,

another feeling of a more delicate sort, so described either because one can enjoy it longer without satiation and exhaustion; or because it presupposes a sensitivity of the soul, so to speak, which makes the soul fitted for virtuous impulses; or because it indicates talents and intellectual excellences.[7]

It is as modes of such 'finer feeling' that we experience the sublime and the beautiful. Again Kant plies us with examples. Mountains with peaks above the clouds, descriptions of raging storms, Milton's portrayal of hell, all arouse 'enjoyment but with horror'; whereas flower-strewn meadows, valleys with winding brooks, or descriptions of Elysium occasion a 'joyous and smiling'

---

[4] Kant, *Observations*, 45.   [5] Ibid. 45.   [6] Ibid. 46.
[7] Ibid. 46. Kant's notion of feeling 'of a more delicate sort' is strongly reminiscent of Addison's description of 'innocent pleasures' in no. 411 of the *Spectator* essays on the Pleasures of the Imagination. Indeed Kant's placing of finer feeling between the pleasures of sense and those of 'high intellectual insights' parallels a similar placement in the Addison essay just mentioned.

Now, 'In order that the former impression [i.e.
with horror] could occur to us in due strength, we
feeling of the sublime, and, in order to enjoy the latter
joyous, smiling, sensation] well, a *feeling of the*

On these terms, in order to enjoy the appropriate states of pleasure, we must have a *disposition* for the sublime and the beautiful. In the case of the sublime, Kant goes on to suggest that our disposition towards it is made occurrent in three characteristic ways. As he puts it,

Its feeling is sometimes accompanied with a certain dread, or melancholy; in some cases merely with quiet wonder; and in still others with a beauty completely pervading a sublime plan. The first I shall call the *terrifying sublime*, the second the *noble*, and the third the *splendid*.[9]

As examples of these, Kant cites (amongst others) great depths as terrifying, great heights as noble, and great buildings (such as the Pyramids) as splendid.

Rather than consider Kant's many other examples of things which engage our feelings of the sublime and beautiful, I shall concentrate on just one of these—discussed in Chapter 2 of the *Observations*. Kant suggests that moral qualities such as sympathy, friendliness, and honour are 'amiable and beautiful' because they can 'harmonise' with (i.e. facilitate) virtue. But while such qualities may help dispose us towards virtue, they are by no means constitutive of it. For example, sympathy for a needy person's plight may lead us into an act of charity that makes us forgo the repayment of a debt. In this case, Kant sees our 'higher obligation' as 'sacrificed' to mere good-natured concern. However,

when universal affection towards the human species has become a principle within you to which you always subordinate your actions, then love towards the needy one remains; but now from a higher standpoint, it has been placed in its true relation to your total duty. Universal affection is a ground of your interest in his plight, but also of the justice by whose rule you must forbear this action.[10]

---

[8] Kant, *Observations*, 46.

[9] Ibid. 47–8. Again, the combination of the sublime and the beautiful in terms of the 'splendid' parallels a similar move in Addison's essay no. 412. Burke, it is interesting to note, was much more reticent about the possibilities of such a combination.   [10] Ibid. 58.

Thus for Kant, while moral virtue presuppos\
affection for humanity, this feeling only takes on i\
moral character when it issues in impartial principle\
rather than *ad hoc* sympathetic responses. It is, inde\
subduing of immediate impulse through principle v\
finds sublime. As he puts it, 'as soon as this feeling o\
for humanity has arisen to its proper universality it ha ⌣ecome
sublime, but also colder.'[11] I shall consider the reason why Kant
finds this universality 'sublime' a little further on.

This brings us to the end of Kant's main philosophical points.
The remainder of the *Observations* is for the most part concerned
with the application of these points to questions such as the
nature of human character-types, the relation between the sexes,
and the characters of different nations. I shall not concern myself
with these questions, but will instead go on to discuss some of
the issues raised by Kant's philosophical points. First, it is
possible that Kant was at least indirectly familiar with Burke's
theory through an extended review of the *Inquiry* written by
Mendelssohn in 1758.[12] However, the differences between the
two theories are quite striking. This is, I would suggest,
not due simply to Burke taking a systematic, and Kant
taking an informal, approach; rather it hinges upon important
philosophical differences. Burke, for instance, holds that the
sublime is essentially a passion of modified terror or pain and
pertains, thereby, to the instinct for self-preservation. While he
takes the subjective aspect of this passion as his starting-point, he
ultimately construes it as the *causal* effect of quite specific
properties in objects. Kant, in contrast, asserts his independence
from this view in the very first sentence of the *Observations*. It
is not the properties of objects so much as the subjective capacity
for feeling which determines the nature of our pleasurable or
displeasurable responses. This allows him to find a greater
diversity both in the employment of our feeling of the sublime,
and in the objects and situations which can occasion it. For
example, our response can embody 'quiet wonder' and the
exhilaration of the 'splendid' as well as delightful horror.
Similarly, it can be occasioned by such things as Friendship,

[11] Ibid. 58.
[12] For a discussion of this, see the Editor's Introduction to Edmund Burke, op. cit.
(n. 2 above), p. cxxv.

Understanding, and Virtue, as well as the more obvious 'sublime' phenomena such as raging storms, and the like. Indeed, for Kant 'sublime' can be a predicate ascribed not simply to the effects akin to terror of other persons and things upon us, but to actions undertaken by ourselves, out of, say, friendship or virtue—and which involve no risk to our physical well-being. This marks a crucial, and (from the point of view of Kant's mature theory) decisive, advance upon Burke.

In marking out these differences between Burke, and Kant's early theory, I am, in effect, denying Mary Mothersill's recent claim that the latter 'draws very heavily'[13] upon the former. However, John Boulton has suggested that 'certain isolated observations and phrases, point unmistakably to Burke's influence'[14] upon the *Observations*. This idea of more piecemeal influence is more difficult to deny. It is, nevertheless, interesting that most of the examples with which Boulton illustrates his claim (such as high mountains, raging storms, Milton's portrayal of Hell, and infinity) are also to be found in a modified form in Addison. The influence of Addison upon Kant[15] has never been adequately studied, but, as I have indicated in some of the notes to this section, many of Kant's ideas in the *Observations* are also to be found in Addison's *Spectator* essays on the Pleasures of Imagination. Given also the fact that Kant mentions the *Spectator* by name, late on in the *Observations*, I would suggest that the piecemeal affinities between Kant and Burke's texts are probably due to common source material.

Let me now consider a second major issue raised by Kant's treatment of the sublime. For a long time in the English-speaking world, our view of Kant's pre-Critical work has been strongly influenced by P. A. Schillp's *Kant's Pre-Critical Ethics*. In this work, Schillp holds fundamentally that Kant was not a moral sense advocate in the manner, say, of Hutcheson. The following passage referring to the *Observations* sums up Schillp's position well.

nowhere in all these references to the 'moral feeling' or 'feeling for morality' . . . does there seem to be any reason for assuming that Kant

---

[13] In her *Beauty Restored* (Clarendon Press: Oxford, 1984), 234.

[14] The Editor's Introduction to Burke, op. cit. (n. 2 above), p. cxxvi.

[15] Addison's *Spectator* essays on the Pleasures of the Imagination were translated into German in 1745.

meant by the term a definitely independent 'sense' or separate 'instinct' such as the British moralists had in mind . . . Indeed there is a remark in the *Beobachtungen* which furnishes no small piece of evidence to the contrary. 'Feeling is in no sense all of a piece' . . . is an assertion of the variety of feelings and, as such, is inconsistent with the British moralists' doctrine of a distinct and unique moral sense.[16]

The most, indeed, that Schillp is prepared to admit is that 'Kant agrees with his British and French tutors upon the importance for the moral life of feeling and of the emotional elements in general'.[17] In relation to Kant's remark about feeling not being 'all of a piece' (leaving aside the fact that Schillp quotes it out of context), there is nothing in it which would count against the possibility of there being a distinct moral sense. A theorist such as Hutcheson does not hold that all feeling is moral, but rather that there are several varieties of feeling (or internal 'senses') of which the moral is one. If Schillp had directly compared Kant and Hutcheson's views he would have actually found them to be almost identical. For example (as we have seen), when Kant talks about the feeling of the sublime, and feeling for morality, he uses the term 'feeling' to denote, not our particular state of quiet wonder, or affection for humanity (or whatever), but rather our disposition to experience such states. Now consider the following passage where Hutcheson sets out his notions of the 'sense of beauty' and the 'moral sense':

These determinations to be pleased with any forms, or ideas which occur to our observation, are what the author [i.e. Hutcheson himself] chooses to call senses, distinguishing them from the powers which commonly go by that name, by calling our power of perceiving the beauty of regularity, order, harmony, an internal sense. And the determination to be pleased with the contemplation of those affections, actions, or characters of rational agents which we call virtuous is what he marks by the name of a moral sense.[18]

Hutcheson's definition of an internal sense as 'a determination to be pleased with' is what in modern philosophical parlance would

---

[16] P. A. Schillp, *Kant's Pre-Critical Ethics* (Northwestern University Press: Evanston, Ill., 1960), 60.

[17] Ibid. 60–1.

[18] Francis Hutcheson, 'An Initial Theory of Taste', in George Dickie and Richard Sclafani (eds.), *Aesthetics: A Critical Anthology* (St Martin's Press: New York, 1977), 569–91. This reference p. 570.

be called a disposition, and could (with only slight grammatical modification) be fitted into almost all those contexts where Kant talks of 'a feeling of', *without any change of meaning taking place.*[19] I am suggesting, therefore, that Kant's treatment of the sublime and the beautiful as feelings in the *Observations* parallels, and is probably influenced by, Hutcheson's notion of an 'internal sense'. Surprisingly, the one point which Schillp does see Kant as having in common with Hutcheson *et al.* (i.e. 'the importance for the moral life of feeling and of the emotional life in general') is one which is in fact somewhat at odds with the new direction which Kant's thought is beginning to take in the *Observations*. For, as we have seen, while Kant sees a feeling of affection for humanity as a presupposition of virtue, he construes 'true virtue' as a special employment of this feeling—namely acting in accordance with universal principles irrespective of our spontaneous emotional impulses.

To conclude this section, I shall now briefly and critically relate Kant's theory to that twofold root of the sublime outlined in Section I of this chapter. First, it is clear that Kant cannot be straightforwardly termed a self-preservation theorist. For while, with Burke, he does allow a state of modified terror to be one form of our feeling of the sublime, he does not advocate that causal theory which enables Burke to construe modified terror and pain and (thereby) a link with self-preservation as the sublime's definitive feature. Whatever defects Burke's causal theory may have, it does at least offer an explanation of what things give rise to the sublime feeling and why they do so. Kant, however, offers no such explicit account, and thence leaves a number of important questions unanswered. Why does our feeling of the sublime dispose us to be moved by such disparate things as precipices, virtue, and pyramids? Why are such disparate emotional states as enjoyment with horror, quiet wonder, and a sense of the splendid to be taken as occurrent instances of the same feeling? These two questions are not

[19] Indeed, it is interesting that, in his *An Inquiry into the Original of Our Ideas of Beauty and Virtue*, Hutcheson points out that 'Grandeur' is an idea which differs from Beauty, though he does not elaborate upon the nature of the difference. Given that the weight of Kant's exposition in the *Observations* falls upon the sublime, it may be that he was consciously trying to fill a gap which Hutcheson had left. This claim is given added plausibility by the fact that Hutcheson's *Inquiry* was translated into German in 1762.

unrelated, in that (from a modern philosophical perspective) to answer the latter, we must, logically speaking, be able to answer the former. The beginnings of such an answer are present in Kant's text, in so far as all the objects and phenomena which he sees as giving rise to the sublime are ones which exercise powers of *non-coercive* physical and/or intellectual authority over us. The deep precipice has the potential to destroy us; true virtue asserts itself as an obligation and duty transcending personal inclination; the pyramid manifests the superiority of collective physical endeavour, and creative genius, over the mundane individual's talents. Kant, in other words, implicitly construes the sublime as occasioned by powers which transcend the self, in some specifiable way. What unites these phenomenologically disparate states of enjoyment with horror, quiet wonder, and a sense of the splendid is that they constitute a mode of reverence. Yet this invites the question of why our reverence for that which has authority over us should be in any sense a source of pleasure—rather than of mere reverence as such. The case of virtue which transcends personal inclination provides an important clue. Here we have something which, in its orientation towards the universal, exceeds our normal sensuous mode of being, but which is not—as a precipice or pyramid is—something external to us. As I shall show (in Chapter 2) of this study), it is by grounding the sublime in such self-transcendence from the sensuous level of our being to the universal that Kant arrives at the basis of his mature theory.[20] Before we can address this question, however, we must finally note some of the important developments which characterize the 'Critical' phase of his philosophy.

III

Kant's mature 'Critical' philosophy is first articulated in the *Critique of Pure Reason* (1781, revised 1787). In this work, Kant

---

[20] Kant's series of lectures on *Anthropology* contains a discussion of the sublime; they were given over a period dating from before the 'Critical' phase of his philosophy. The version of the lectures published posthumously, however, has clearly been revised on the basis of his Critical position, and their discussion of the sublime is derived substantially from the mature theory outlined in the *Critique of Judgement*.

argues that space and time are not properties of things in themselves, but are 'forms of intuition', that is features inherent in the general constitution of sentient creatures such as ourselves. On these terms, therefore, in so far as space and time are contributed by ourselves, we know a priori that all 'intuitions' (i.e. particular sensible existents) will appear to us as given in space and time. But for Kant cognition is not simply a receptive process. Any manifold of sensible intuition given in space and time is also actively structured by the faculty of understanding with its concepts. Kant's major arguments to this effect centre on the Transcendental Deduction in the *Critique of Pure Reason*. The gist of Kant's position here is that, in the most general terms, an object is a manifold of sensible intuitions which has been combined and unified in terms of some specific 'rule' (i.e. concept). Now such combination or 'synthesis' can itself only be carried out by a unified consciousness, that is one which can be (at least sometimes) aware of itself as distinct from that which it is aware *of*. But, reciprocally, such a consciousness can only be unified in these terms in so far as it synthesizes the manifold of intuitions on the basis of those fundamental rules or 'pure concepts of the understanding' which Kant calls 'categories'. The depth of this reciprocal dependence is best illustrated through the category of causality. In the Second Analogy in the *Critique of Pure Reason*, for example, Kant argues that, if we are to distinguish statements about our *own* 'representations' (i.e. our present awareness of sensible objects, or our acts of recollecting or imagining or thinking of such objects) from statements about the objects *themselves*, then we must say that (as A. C. Ewing succinctly puts it), 'the latter sort of statements gives an account of what any other normal observer would see under given conditions, and this is to assert a causal law governing human perceptions.'[21]

On these terms, the category of causality and the laws of nature which embody it are fundamental in enabling us to draw a distinction between an objective order of events and the subjective experience of these.

It must be noted, however, that, while we can have objective knowledge of the phenomenal world, we cannot have such

[21] A. C. Ewing, *A Short Commentary on Kant's* Critique of Pure Reason (Methuen: London, 1938), 162.

knowledge of that 'noumenal' or 'supersensible' substratum which provides the material from which the understanding's categories and the forms of intuition constitute phenomenal experience. That there *is* such a realm follows from Kant's overall philosophical position, but since, by definition, it transcends the bounds of what can be experienced it cannot form an object of knowledge for theoretical reason. This division between the phenomenal and noumenal also extends to the human self. For, on the one hand, we are embodied creatures of feeling and sensibility, who think and act in time and space. This means that as phenomenal beings we are a part of nature and are subject to determination by nature's causal laws. On the other hand, in so far as it is the human subject which imposes this causal network through the categories of understanding and the forms of intuition, the ultimate ground of the self must in some sense be presumed to lie beyond the phenomenal world. It must, in other words, be a noumenal or supersensible self. Now this area of Kant's philosophy is, unfortunately, deeply problematic, inasmuch as the relations between the phenomenal self, the formal unity of consciousness, and the supersensible self are never adequately clarified by him. Indeed, in terms of consistency with his overall Critical epistemology Kant can only give the supersensible self a negative characterization—namely as that aspect of the self which is not in space and time, and not subject to the categories. However, in the realm of goal-orientated human activity—'practical reason'—Kant holds that there are grounds for a much more positive characterization. His justification for this view consists in the fact that in the practical sphere our actions involve the exercise of *free will* on the basis of rational principles, rather than purely mechanical determination by that natural causality which arises from the application of the categories. This exercise of free will is embodied in 'pure practical reason' (i.e. morality). In this case (according to Kant) not only are our decisions motivated by rational principles alone (rather than by sensuous inclinations such as the desire for happiness) but they often involve us acting contrarily to those sensuous impulses which most emphatically locate us in the mechanistic framework of nature. In fact the very existence of morality (a fact which Kant takes as given) presupposes a rational and autonomous dimension to the self. For if our decisions were always merely mechanically determined, then it would make no sense—in the way that morality demands—for us to hold people responsible for their actions, and to assign praise and blame accordingly. On these terms, the supersensible self must be presumed to be both rational and free.

Having outlined two salient eighteenth-century theories of the sublime and Kant's own theory, and having also noted some of the crucial claims which characterize Kant's Critical philosophy, we can now attend to his Critical theory of the sublime.

2

Kant's Critical Ethics and the Sublime

Kant's first formulation of his mature theory of the sublime is to be found in the *Groundwork of the Metaphysic of Morals* (1785) and the *Critique of Practical Reason* (1788). In order to understand this theory, I shall begin with a more detailed exposition of Kant's position on morality.

First, we will remember from the preceding chapter that, for Kant, moral decision is inaugurated by the rational and autonomous supersensible self. It is, however, important to note that, because the rational self is conjoined with a phenomenal counterpart, the latter tends to inhibit the workings of the former. This means that the principles which inform our moral decisions are influenced by potentially distracting feelings and desires, and we can, in consequence, only act in an imperfectly rational way. We do not (as a wholly rational being would) necessarily adopt the principle of action which the realization of some specific end objectively demands.[1] This is why Kant holds that our willing of ends is always expressible in the form of hypothetical or categorical *imperatives*. The former are conditional, and take the form of 'If I want x, then I ought to do y'. In such cases our principle of action is determined by an end that is contingent upon a particular desire (i.e. an end derived from our phenomenal being). A categorical imperative, in contrast, is unconditional, and simply takes the form 'I ought to do y'. Here our principle of action is determined fundamentally not by some empirical end, but by the demands of reason itself. As Kant puts it:

It is concerned, not with the matter of the action and its presumed results, but with its form and with the principle from which it follows: and what is essentially good in the action consists in the mental disposition, let the consequences be what they may. This imperative may be called the imperative of *morality*.[2]

---

[1] Cf. the discussion of error at B50/A294 in *Pure Reason*, 293.

[2] Kant, *Groundwork*, 84.

All the principles of morality (according to Kant) are expressible in the single categorical imperative, 'Act only on that maxim through which you can at the same time will that it should become a universal law'.[3] This means, in practice, that a judgement only has moral validity if it is universally and necessarily binding on us, by virtue of our status as rational beings alone. For example, the principle 'always make sincere promises' counts as a genuine moral demand, in so far as any exception to it (i.e. the making of a lying promise) would—if made a principle of action—be irrational, through being at odds with (as Kant puts it) 'the very purpose of promising'.[4]

For the purposes of the present study, it is not necessary to survey the many interesting questions which Kant's views raise. I shall be content instead to note the single crucial point that, while the moral law is binding on us absolutely, it is in no sense alien and external to us; rather it is legislated by our supersensible rational being and is testimony to our ultimate vocation—namely to engage in free responsible action, irreducible to the workings of purely natural causality. With this point in mind, we can now consider the new interpretation of sublimity which Kant offers in the *Groundwork* and *Critique of Practical Reason*. In the former work Kant suggests that it is 'freedom from dependence on interested motives [i.e. ones determined by sensuous impulse] which constitutes the sublimity of a maxim'.[5]

Indeed, we are told further, in relation to the particular moral consciousness, that 'it is not in so far as he is subject to the law that he has sublimity, but rather in so far as, in regard to this very same law, he is at the same time its author'.[6]

Kant is here developing the link between sublimity and morality broached in the *Observations*, but with one important difference. Sublimity is now posited, not primarily in terms of a feeling, but as a predicate ascribed to wills determined by the moral law, that is wills that have transcended determination by any natural impulse (including even sympathy). In the *Critique of Practical Reason* Kant goes so far as to define 'personality' exclusively in terms of such sublime moral consciousness. On the one hand, it is 'freedom and independence from the mechanism of nature',[7] and, on the other hand, the capacity for being 'subject

---

[3] Kant, *Groundwork*, 88.   [4] Ibid. 90.   [5] Ibid. 106.
[6] Ibid. 107.   [7] Kant, *Practical Reason*, 193.

to special laws (pure practical laws given by its own reason)'.[8]
This, in turn, leads to the decisive claim that the idea of
personality 'places before our eyes the sublimity of our nature (in
its [higher] vocation)'.[9]

On these terms, moral consciousness is sublime because it
manifests the ultimate authority and transcendence of our
rational over our sensible being. While this indeed marks a shift
from the *Observations* position—where sublimity is construed
dispositionally, as a feeling—Kant does nevertheless suggest that
sublime moral consciousness embodies a rather privileged kind of
feeling of its own. For example, in the *Groundwork* we are
informed that 'duty is the necessity to act out of respect for the
[moral] law'.[10] Respect is here (stipulatively) defined as a feeling,
but 'not a feeling received through outside influence, [rather] one
self-produced by a rational concept [i.e. the moral law] and
therefore specifically distinct from feelings of the first kind'.[11]

It is important to note that, here, Kant's conception of moral
feeling is the reverse of the position set out in the *Observations*.
Moral consciousness does not start from some affectionate feeling
for humankind which is then generalized into a universal
principle; we find instead that moral feeling (i.e. 'respect') is the
outcome of our recognition that the will is necessarily subject to
the moral law. It arises, in other words, *from* our self-
transcendence towards the universal. Now in the *Groundwork*
Kant also makes the suggestion that

If we are to will actions for which reason by itself prescribes an 'ought' to
a rational, yet sensuously affected, being, it is admittedly necessary that
reason should have a power of infusing a feeling of pleasure or
satisfaction in the fulfilment of duty . . . It is, however, wholly
impossible to comprehend—that is, make intelligible *a priori*—how a

---

[8] Ibid. 193.
[9] Ibid. 194. It is important to note this special sense of personality as that aspect of
us wherein our freedom is exercised in the realization of *universal laws*. Milton
Nahm, in contrast, in his paper 'Sublimity and the Moral Law in Kant's Philosophy'
(*Kant-Studien*, 48 (1957), 504–24) makes the mistake of identifying personality as
that which is unique to us as individual beings (p. 522). He is thus led to make some
unwarranted connections between Kant's notion of morality and the theory of genius
proposed in the third *Critique*.
[10] Kant, *Groundwork*, 68. For purposes of uniformity with other translations,
I shall substitute 'respect' for Paton's preferred translation of *Achtung* as 'reverence'.
[11] Ibid. 128.

mere thought containing nothing sensible in itself can bring about a sensation of pleasure or displeasure.[12]

There are at least two things about this passage which are puzzling. First, given that Kant has gone so far as to define duty as the necessity of acting out of respect for the law, one would have thought that, if it is necessary that reason should give rise to some feeling, then 'respect' would be the obvious candidate— rather than the sense of 'satisfaction' which Kant describes. Second, given that the relationship between 'reason by itself' and feeling cannot be understood in a priori terms, and given also the clear fact that it is not analytic; then in exactly what sense is it 'necessary' that reason should give rise to some sort of feeling?

That Kant became aware of these two questions is shown by the fact that Chapter 3 of the *Critique of Practical Reason* is devoted in large part to an analysis of 'respect', and Kant is led to the view that, in this case at least, the relationship between reason and feeling is necessary in an a priori sense.[13] His discussion proceeds as follows. First, while Kant denies the possibility of an explanation as to how and why the moral law is able to determine the will so as to constitute an incentive for action he is able, nevertheless, to provide a description of the effect which such determination must have upon our feelings. The basic feature of this effect is inhibition—a checking of all those inclinations to self-love and personal interest which are at odds with the law's universality. As he puts it,

the effect of the moral law as an incentive is only negative, and as such this incentive can be known *a priori*. For all inclination and every sensuous impulse is based on feeling, and the negative effect on feeling (through the check on the inclinations) is itself feeling. Consequently, we can see *a priori* that the moral law as a ground of determination of the

---

[12] Kant, *Groundwork*, 128.

[13] Whether this also applies to the feeling of moral satisfaction mentioned in the *Groundwork* is more difficult to determine as, indeed, is the very relation between respect and moral satisfaction. In the course of his 'Critical Resolution of the Antinomy of Practical Reason' in the second *Critique* (221–2) Kant suggests that, whereas respect is a *feeling* directly occurrent upon determination of our will by the moral law, moral satisfaction or 'self-contentment' is a *state of mind* that characterizes our following of the moral law with 'an unyielding *disposition* [my italics]'. For a discussion of some of the complex related issues involved here see George Schrader's 'The Status of Feeling in Kant's Philosophy', *Proceedings of the International Kant Congress 1974*. 143–64.

will, by thwarting all our inclinations, must produce a feeling which can be called pain.[14]

On these terms, because the moral law is a check upon our inclinations, it must modify them by giving rise to another feeling. Kant now goes on to describe this from a somewhat broader perspective. The pursuit of happiness, and even selfishness, he admits, is always active in us, and is merely temporarily checked by the moral law. However, 'self-conceit'—stipulatively defined as the view that features contingent upon the human condition (such as happiness, or other-regarding emotions such as sympathy) constitute the supreme principle of morality—is something which determination by the moral law 'strikes down' and 'humiliates' altogether. It is by the thwarting of sensible impulses and the principles unwarrantably derived from such impulses that a feeling akin to pain is produced. But this negative effect has two rewarding consequences. First, by checking and humiliating our impulses and 'self-conceit' it clears away obstacles to authentic moral decision, that is, makes it easier for our will to be determined by the moral law on future occasions. Second, it reinforces our awareness that that which has destroyed our 'self-conceit' is an 'intellectual causality' (i.e. a manifestation of our wholly rational supersensible self). The feeling akin to pain thus serves to elevate us with a sense of our ultimate rational vocation. In Kant's words, 'respect for the law is . . . by virtue of its intellectual cause a positive feeling that can be known *a priori*'.[15]

The difficulties raised by Kant's notion of respect are legion. It has, for example, been found problematic in relation to the role he assigns it in the motivation of moral decisions.[16] For the purposes of the present study, however, there are rather more pressing critical and interpretative issues to be raised. The first of these (surprisingly neglected by some commentators[17]) is very important for Kant's discussion of sublimity in the third

---

[14] *Practical Reason*, 181.   [15] Ibid. 186.

[16] These and related difficulties are plausibly answered by L. W. Beck in his *A Commentary on Kant's 'Critique of Practical Reason'* (University of Chicago Press: Chicago, 1969), 221–5.

[17] Such as e.g. Beck and Schrader (both op. cit., nn. 13, 16). H. J. Paton's neglect of the issue in his *The Categorical Imperative* (Hutchinson: London, 1953) is more understandable in so far as that study focuses mainly on the *Groundwork*—where (as I have shown) Kant was more uncertain as to the status of respect.

Critique. It hinges on Kant's causal justification of respect's claim
to a priori status. We will recall that, since consciousness of the
moral law checks our contrary inclinations, it 'must' do so by
producing a negative feeling that humiliates our 'self-conceit'
and, in turn, serves to elevate us with a sense of our supersensible
rational vocation. But why 'must' it do so? Might not the moral
law's direct inhibition of contrary impulses simply take the form
of a vague sense of conscious restraint? Indeed, might we not
develop a disposition for suppressing inclinations contrary to the
law's demands? In such a case, our habitual conformity to the
moral law would surely enable it to determine the will without
involving an *occurrent* feeling of respect on every such occasion.

Now it may be that any unease Kant felt on this score
concerning the necessity of respect was more than compensated
for by a consideration bound up with the demands of his
overall philosophical position. It is fundamental to Kant's
transcendental idealism that all events—including human decisions
and actions—can be sufficiently accounted for in terms of
causal explanations derived from laws of nature. This seems
immediately incompatible with his commitment to freedom of
the will. But Kant himself felt that the two views were, in fact,
compatible—though his justification of this claim is somewhat
complex. One might attempt to sketch it in outline as follows. If
we are sufficiently to account for all our deeds and actions in
terms of natural causality, then we must be able to explain them
in terms of motives derived from sensuous impulses and feelings.
If this account is to leave room for the exercise of morality and
free will—but without bringing them directly into the causal
story—then we must presume that the moral law's determination
of the will involves some phenomenal counterpart (i.e. a sensible
state) which *can* figure as a kind of proxy for moral motivation in
the explanation derived from natural causality. Respect is just
this phenomenal counterpart. Hence, if we wished to explain in
terms of natural causality why some person makes a moral
decision, we would trace its origins to a feeling of respect.
Conversely, if we wished to explain why a person failed to make
some moral decision, we would trace it to a state where the
feeling of respect failed to displace contrary sensuous impulses.
On these terms, the determination of the will by the moral law
'must' involve an occurrent feeling of respect because it is only on

this presupposition that the determination of human agency by natural causality *and* the possibility of free moral agency are rendered compatible.

Now while considerations of this sort may inform Kant's treatment of respect, such an approach is, nevertheless, deeply problematic. For if our explanations of human motivation and agency in terms of natural causality are fully to satisfy conditions of sufficiency (and, as we shall see later, Kant regards this demand as essential), then there will come a point when we will have to ask *why* respect arises. The answer to this question will break the chain of explanation in terms of natural causality alone. I would argue, therefore, that, since Kant's claim that respect is a necessary outcome of moral decision does not facilitate a successful compatibilist argument, there is no philosophical compulsion to assign a priori status to it. In fact, even if we did allow the claim that moral decision does necessarily give rise to some feeling, problems would still remain. These hinge on the complex structure which Kant assigns to the feeling of respect. It has a first stage where pain gives rise to the humiliation of 'self-conceit', and a second positive stage of elevation arising from an awareness of morality as our ultimate vocation. However, in relation to the negative aspect, might this not simply involve a feeling of pain or frustration *as such*? In deeply moral persons, of course, the humiliation of 'self-conceit' may be bound up with this, but those whose moral susceptibilities are less well articulated may obey the voice of moral conscience in relation to particular situations without even beginning to countenance the humiliating general implications which it has for egoism as a world-view. Indeed, while such a person might recognize and act on the authority of the moral law, he or she might also lack the clarity of insight which leads on to the positive aspect of respect, that is a sense of morality as our ultimate vocation. In fact, even if Kant were to insist on some positive aspect as being necessarily involved in respect (in so far as it provides a phenomenal motive for morality), there is no necessity that it should be the sense of elevation which he describes. (It could, for example, equally well be that feeling of moral satisfaction which is mentioned in the *Groundwork*.) I am arguing that, even if we allow Kant the claim that moral decision necessarily causes a complex feeling, he must nevertheless allow that the form which its negative and positive aspects take will be determined by levels of moral susceptibility and insight contingent upon the individual moral agent. On these terms, if we show extreme charity to Kant, he might claim a priori status for some form of complex moral feeling as such—but not for that specific complex structure which he calls respect.[18]

The second major question raised for this study by Kant's notion of respect is fundamentally interpretative. In the *Groundwork* and the second *Critique* the only occasions on which Kant uses the term 'sublime' are in relation to the determination of the will by the moral law—which (as I have just shown) is taken by him necessarily to involve the feeling of respect. Now is Kant's narrow usage of 'sublime' here merely incidental, or does it reflect the fact that he now regards moral consciousness alone as sublime, and that, in consequence, respect alone is the authentic feeling of sublimity? The following passage from the second *Critique* is instructive here.

Respect always applies to persons [i.e. beings determinable by the moral law] only, never to things. The latter can awaken inclinations, and even love if they are animals . . . or fear, as do the sea, a volcano, or a beast of prey; but they never arouse respect. Something which approaches this feeling is admiration, and this, as an effect (astonishment) can also refer to things, lofty mountains, the magnitude, number, and distance of the heavenly bodies, the strength and swiftness of many animals. All of this, however, is not respect.[19]

What is remarkable about this passage is that, while it provides an obvious context for talk of 'sublimity', we find, nevertheless, that those sorts of physical objects which in the *Observations* Kant describes as giving rise to the feeling of the sublime are here emphatically presented only in terms of fear and admiration or astonishment. Indeed he is at great pains to separate such states from that feeling of respect which arises from sublime moral consciousness. This, I would suggest, is indicative of the fact that he now wishes to reserve the term sublime exclusively for the moral domain. It might be objected that this is an overstatement and that Kant is doing little more than reassert his position in the

---

[18] For a further example of Kant drawing unwarranted psychological conclusions from fundamentally logical premisses, see the discussion of his Deduction of taste in Chapter 3, Section III, of this study.

[19] *Practical Reason*, 184.

Observations. There, it will be remembered, Kant construes the feeling of the sublime as a disposition which is made occurrent in three characteristic ways—enjoyment with horror, quiet wonder, and a sense of the splendid. Could we not, therefore, view the second *Critique*'s trichotomy of fear, respect, and admiration or amazement as simply repeating the earlier distinctions in a slightly modified way? On these terms, respect would be that state which is made occurrent when our feeling for the sublime is engaged in a moral context. The easy response to this is to look ahead to the *Critique of Judgement* (1790). Here the superiority of moral consciousness, and its feeling of respect, is explicitly made the basis of sublimity as such. As Kant puts it, even 'the feeling of the sublime in nature is respect for our own vocation . . . this feeling renders, as it were, intuitable the supremacy of our faculties on the rational side over the greatest faculty of sensibility'.[20]

I shall describe in detail why Kant feels able to ground an aesthetic theory of the sublime on moral consciousness in Part II of my study. But it is worth noting now that the grounds on which Kant would feel justified in making a stipulative link between sublimity and moral consciousness are already present in his Critical ethics. Let us consider why Kant should imagine that moral consciousness is so *uniquely* worthy of the term 'sublime'. The basis of an answer is already apparent to some degree from the foregoing. In the pre-Critical *Observations* Kant regards as sublime those objects which engage our disposition for sublimity through (as I put it earlier) their exertion of a non-coercive authority over us. However, in his critical phase it would have struck Kant that the authority of such things as precipices, principles derived from sympathy, and pyramids extends to our phenomenal being alone, that is, it is only at the level of embodied sensibility, with its fears, inclinations, and limited perceptual capacities, that such things as the above can be regarded as threatening, or transcendent. But from the viewpoint of the supersensible self no phenomenal item can claim such authority. Our supersensible being is beyond space and time, and is not subject to mechanistic determination by natural causality. Indeed, it is able to bring about changes in the phenomenal world

---

[20] *Judgement*, 176–7.

(even against our natural inclinations) solely on the basis of its own principles. Hence, for Kant, the supersensible grounding of moral consciousness renders it ontologically superior to any phenomenal object or state.

There are also two further ways (following on from the above) in which moral consciousness can be regarded as superior to any item in the phenomenal world. In the *Groundwork* Kant claims that 'It is impossible to conceive anything at all in the world, or even out of it, which can be taken as good without qualification, except a *good will*.'[21]

The reasoning which underpins this claim hinges on two broad points. First, whenever the term 'good' is used in relation to a phenomenal state, quality, or object it is conditional on the particular context in which such items occur. For example, while such things as power, wealth, and happiness are normally regarded as good, we would not (in Kant's terms) regard them as thus if they characterized the social standing and well-being of a sadistic torturer.[22] Here, the context in which such prima-facie goods occur would serve to render them undesirable. Second, our use of the term 'good' in relation to phenomenal items other than moral consciousness is contingent on human nature (i.e. that of a finite imperfectly rational creature). In contrast, a wholly rational being not subject to sensuous inclinations would place no value on such items; it might even regard them as bad, in so far as they distract and inhibit such finite creatures as we from being wholly rational. Linking these two points together (and overlooking the many questions they raise), it is clear that only the moral law—binding on all rational beings in all contexts by virtue of their rationality—can lay claim to the status of unconditional worth. I shall, therefore, call this the *axiological* superiority of moral consciousness.

As we have seen, for Kant moral consciousness is grounded on our rationally autonomous supersensible being. However, he also feels that it involves two further presuppositions. These are introduced through the notion of the 'highest good'. In relation to this, we are told that

---

[21] *Groundwork*, 61.
[22] This example is not Kant's but it parallels his point in the *Groundwork* (62) that the villain's coolheadedness makes him all the more reprehensible.

virtue (as the [moral] worthiness to be happy) is the supreme condition of whatever appears to us to be desirable and thus of all our pursuit of happiness . . . But these truths do not imply that it is in the entire and perfect good as the object of the faculty of desire of rational finite beings.[23]

Kant's point here is that, while the moral law is the overriding condition of practical reason as such, we must, nevertheless, acknowledge that in finite rational beings practical reason also encompasses the realizing of ends which we expect (directly or indirectly) to bring us happiness. Hence, taking account of both our rational and sensuous dimensions (i.e. the totality of our being), the 'highest good' which a practical finite being can hope for is a harmonious combination of virtue and happiness. For Kant this means specifically that we must necessarily aspire towards happiness that is in proportion to (i.e. does not outweigh) our moral worth. In order to establish the conditions which are presupposed in order for this highest good to be attainable Kant outlines two 'postulates of pure practical reason'—the first of which relates to the moral component alone, and the second of which pertains to the relation between morality and happiness. Kant argues the first of these as follows. In this life we cannot hope to achieve a perfect congruence between our will and the moral law—even though this is what the moral law enjoins us do.

But since it [perfect congruence] is required as practically necessary, it can be found only in an endless progress to that complete fitness; on principles of pure practical reason, it is necessary to assume such a practical progress as the real object of our will.

This infinite progress is possible, however, only under the presupposition of an infinitely enduring existence and personality of the same rational being.[24]

On these terms, given that the moral law demands the possibility of its own perfect realization (and thence necessarily involves the assumption of the immortality of the soul) and given also that the moral law constitutes the major pre-condition of the highest good, it follows that the highest good presupposes the assumption of the immortality of the soul. Kant then proceeds to his second postulate as follows: 'there is not the slightest ground

[23] *Practical Reason*, 215.   [24] Ibid. 225–6.

in the moral law [itself] for a necessary connection between the morality and proportionate happiness of a being which belongs to the world.'[25]

Hence, to establish the possibility of this 'necessary' connection, we must postulate the existence 'of a cause of the whole of nature, itself distinct from nature, which contains the ground of the exact coincidence of happiness with morality'.[26]

We must suppose, in other words, the existence of a just and benevolent God who has created the world so as to provide for the possibility of the highest good being realized. Given that the moral sphere leads us to affirm the existence not only of freedom, but also of an immortal soul and God, one might say that this renders it cosmologically superior to any aspect of the phenomenal world.

Clearly Kant's arguments for the ontological, axiological, and cosmological superiority of moral consciousness are, to say the least, of debatable value. Yet the fact that he sees morality in this light explains why he would feel justified in regarding moral consciousness alone as worthy of the term sublime. This threefold superiority also provides material to deal with a further important interpretative issue raised by Geoffrey Warnock. To understand this issue, we must now consider some broader points (which will also be relevant to subsequent chapters of this study). First (as we have seen), the ultimate grounding of morality's authority over us lies in our status as rational beings. However, for Kant, as well as exercising reason in a practical sense we also exercise it in a theoretical mode. Now it is important to be clear about what the latter involves. In this respect we will again remember that it is through the combined function of the forms of intuition, and the pure categories of understanding, that the possibility of experience is established. It is through the understanding's organization of sensible intuitions that we are able to distinguish particular objects and events, and (as the Second Analogy in the first *Critique* in particular shows) relate these to one another on the basis of universally valid causal laws. Early on in the first *Critique* Kant uses the term 'reason' in its theoretical sense, to encompass this general activity of the understanding. But in the Transcendental Dialectic he treats

[25] *Practical Reason*, 228.   [26] Ibid. 228.

'reason' as a more specialized employment of the understanding. Its specific function is to formulate 'principles', that is concepts which seek to systematize and unify other sets of concepts. The reason why Kant introduces this special definition has been pointed out very succinctly by J. F. Macfarland.

Within nature as a system in accordance with the categorical principles, we find a possibly infinite diversity of individual substances, causal relations, and mutual interactions amongst substances.[27]

Our categorical knowledge of the world, in other words, provides a framework wherein there still remains a teeming multiplicity of particular items and relations whose existence and order stand in need of explanation. In relation to such items of empirical knowledge, Kant asserts that we demand that our explanations of them should be so systematic and complete as to be *unconditional* (i.e. incapable of being explained in terms of further, still more general, principles). This demand constitutes what Kant calls the 'interest' of theoretical reason. He outlines its workings (in the first *Critique*) as follows.

If we consider in its whole range the [empirical] knowledge obtained for us by the understanding, we find that what is peculiarly distinctive of reason in its attitude to this body of knowledge is that it prescribes and seeks to achieve its *systematisation*, that is, to exhibit the connection of its parts in conformity with a single principle . . . This idea [of theoretical reason] accordingly postulates a complete unity in the knowledge obtained by the understanding, by which this knowledge is to be not a mere contingent aggregate, but a system connected according to necessary laws.[28]

On these terms, while (with our finite intellects) we cannot discover the ultimate systematizing connections between those bodies of empirical knowledge furnished by the understanding, the interest of theoretical reason nevertheless demands systematic and necessary unity. We are led, therefore, to employ a priori regulative principles ('ideas of reason') in order to achieve such systematization. Consider the notion of 'substance' in relation to the self. In the Transcendental Dialectic of the first *Critique* Kant argues that we cannot know whether the self really is a

[27] J. F. Macfarland, *Kant's Concept of Teleology* (Edinburgh University Press: Edinburgh, 1970), 15.
[28] A645/B673, p. 534.

substance or not. However, used as a regulative idea of reason in the field of empirical psychology, the assumption that the self *is* in fact a substance provides a convenient methodological device for systematically understanding the relation between different aspects of the phenomenal self. Hence, while the pure concepts of understanding guarantee that we have general objective knowledge of the world, there remains, as it were, a surplus of particular kinds of empirical knowledge whose further systematic articulation necessitates the use of another kind of a priori principle. It is in order to pick out these latter a priori regulative principles that Kant introduces the distinction between understanding and reason.

Given this a priori significance which Kant assigns to theoretical reason, Geoffrey Warnock has asked[29] why he does not regard it as so awe-inspiring and worthy of respect as moral reason (or, to frame the question in terms of the present study, why should the term sublime not be used in relation to theoretical reason as well as to morality)? According to Warnock, in the second *Critique* Kant addresses this issue in two extremely unsatisfactory ways. I shall consider these and Warnock's objections to them in turn. First, Warnock rightly points out that Kant is extremely impressed by the fact that through morality's grounding in rational autonomy we are able to act independently of mechanical or quasi-mechanical determination by natural causality. But Warnock suggests that this is not essentially different from theoretical reason:

For in the exercise of theoretical reason . . . we are, or at least we are no less inclined to suppose that we are able to think, to believe, to argue, to conclude, in the light of what we take to be reasons for so doing, and do not merely slide, as it were, from thought to thought in sequences capable only of causal explanation.[30]

Indeed, even if Kant stresses the fact that in moral consciousness the will acts independently of, and even against, our 'natural' inclinations, the same can be true of theoretical reason. As Warnock puts it,

We may be reluctant to believe things no less than to do things. Just as we may find that there are reasons for doing what we would much prefer

---

[29] In the essay 'The Primacy of Practical Reason' included in his book *Morality and Language* (Basil Blackwell: Oxford, 1982).

[30] Ibid. 184.

not to, we may find that there are reasons for thinking what we would much prefer not to think.[31]

The problem with Warnock's approach is that having initially acknowledged Kant's quite specialized use of the term 'theoretical reason' (as the striving for unconditional knowledge) he goes on, nevertheless, to treat it as though it were synonymous with reasoning in the broadest sense of that term.[32] But if we bear in mind Kant's particular usage of 'theoretical reason', Warnock's objection can be answered within Kant's overall philosophical frame of reference. In this respect, we should first note that, while the exercise of theoretical reason (like morality) cannot be accounted for in causal terms, it is restricted in two important ways. First, theoretical reason is (in Kant's terms) 'heteronomous' in so far as through it we prescribe laws for the understanding of that which is other than ourselves (i.e. for nature). In pure practical reason, in contrast, we legislate solely for the conduct of our own being. Hence, whereas, in the former, reason is, in a sense, at the service of cognition—as a means to system and unity in understanding—in the latter reason is employed autonomously for its own sake alone. It is, therefore, morality which is the purest (and therefore ontologically superior) embodiment of our supersensible rational essence. Following on from this, the second way in which theoretical reason is restricted is in terms of the value of its exercise. In the case of morality we are enjoined to strive towards the realization of the moral law unconditionally in all contexts by virtue of our status as rational beings—morality is not something we can (*qua* rational beings) choose to refrain from. No such imperative, however, holds in the case of the employment of theoretical reason. If we wish to bring knowledge to its highest degree of unity, then we must exercise theoretical reason. Yet it may be that a person has no aptitude for such intellectual pursuits. In such a case it would, in Kantian terms, be entirely reasonable for the individual in question to refrain from theoretical reason in favour of interests more conducive to the development of whatever gifts or abilities he or she might have. The value of theoretical reason, in other words, is relative to a context. This point also enables us to deal

---

[31] Ibid. 185.

[32] This reflects a tension in his paper between Kant exegesis and the intention to cast light on why generally we ascribe primacy to moral, over other, forms of value.

with Warnock's observation that as in the case of moral decision we sometimes think, decide, believe (or whatever) against our personal inclinations. Let us ask why we should be so disposed. The answer (a Kantian one, but of more general plausibility) is that our self-regarding impulses here are restricted by a sense of duty towards ourselves and others. Should, for example, some empirical data cast doubt on the validity of a cherished theory, we would accept the unpleasant implications of the data because to do otherwise would count as a cheating of ourselves—that is as a refusal to meet a challenge to our existing beliefs which might develop our powers of rational thinking in new directions. Indeed, if we should not accept the data because of personal inclination and prejudice alone, this might be argued as constituting an infringement of duties owed to others—in the context of our essentially shared commitment to the pursuit of truth. I would suggest, then, that in Kantian terms theoretical reason is exercised against our inclinations only because the motive of such an exercise is a sense of duty owed to oneself and to others. It involves at least an indirect moral motive.

The main reason which Warnock sees as underlying Kant's privileging of practical over theoretical reason is as follows. For Kant, theoretical reason is limited because theoretical arguments cannot demonstrate anything of objective validity about the world unless the object of that demonstration is something which could constitute a possible experience. This rules out any objective knowledge of the supersensible. At best, theoretical reason can only show such Ideas of Reason as Freedom, Immortality, and God (i.e. aspects of the supersensible) to be non-contradictory. However, practical reason takes us beyond this, because (as I showed earlier) the existence of Freedom, Immortality, and God is presupposed by morality. Warnock suggests that these presuppositions are, in fact, a liability. As he puts it:

in the 'practical use' of reason we find ourselves obliged to accept as its preconditions propositions which cannot conceivably be shown to be true, and which otherwise we have no reason whatever to believe. And this seems to say that reason in its practical use lies under the logical disability of leaving, so to speak, intellectual loose ends, of constraining us to accept what we cannot possibly show to be true.[33]

[33] Warnock, op. cit. (n. 29 above), 187.

On these terms, the only reason why moral consciousness turns out to be so eminently worthy of respect is because it involves presuppositions which are morally and spiritually salutary.

But this, of course [Warnock continues], is to assume the conclusion of his own argument—namely that, at any point of divergence between the practical and theoretical uses of reason, it is to its practical use that primacy must be afforded.[34]

This leads Warnock to conclude that not only does Kant fail to establish the primacy of practical reason, but, indeed, we can regard theoretical reason as having the better claim to primacy precisely because it does not burden us with troublesome presuppositions. Warnock's criticisms here are valid only if we take him to be contrasting Kant's notion of practical reason with that of theoretical reason viewed in the *non-Kantian* sense of mere thinking, believing, deciding (or whatever) on the basis of reasons. However, if we remember that for Kant theoretical reason is essentially a striving for unconditional knowledge, then again, within the terms of Kant's own philosophy, matters take on a somewhat different character. The interest of theoretical reason demands that we use Ideas whose truth must be assumed for purposes of enquiry but which are incapable of being theoretically demonstrated. This seems to leave theoretical reason in very much the position which Warnock assigns to Kant's notion of practical reason. But in Kant's terms practical reason can still claim primacy not only because of the ontological and axiological superiority noted earlier, but also because its cosmologically superior presuppositions are, in a sense, required by theoretical reason itself. The justification for this claim lies in Kant's notion of the 'interest' of theoretical reason, that is, the striving for unconditional a priori connections between bodies of knowledge. Let us suppose in this respect that we seek an answer to such ultimate questions as 'Why does the universe exist?' 'Why is it ordered as it is?' 'What is humankind's relation to this purpose and order?' For Kant, such questions cannot be conclusively answered in theoretical terms; but throughout the three *Critiques* he hints that the three Ideas of Reason which relate most directly to morality—namely God, Freedom, and Immortality—can also have a regulative application in relation to

[34] Ibid.

theoretical reason. He does not, it is true, offer much explanation of this function, but the following account would be consistent with his position. The assumed actual existence of God is a notion which is required to account for why the world exists, and why it has the order it does. In turn, the assumption of freedom and immortality is required in order to provide a complete explanation of humankind's place in the cosmological scheme of things. Indeed, in the third *Critique* (as we shall see in the following chapter) Kant quite explicitly links God, the world, and freedom, by claiming that God must be assumed to have created the world so as to allow free beings an arena (as it were) in which to make moral decisions. In conjunction, the three major Ideas of Reason provide regulative principles which can provide an all-embracing theoretical explanation of the world's *raison d'être* and humankind's relation to it. This, however, leads us to the decisive point. For while the interest of theoretical reason will commit us to the use of the Ideas of God, Freedom, and Immortality, in order to provide the most complete explanation of the world, they remain, nevertheless, assumed and methodological truths only—a status that conflicts with theoretical reason's own striving for the unconditional. If, therefore, pure practical reason provides (as it does) grounds for affirming the reality of such ideas then, in effect, it takes the interest or striving which defines theoretical reason one step further, even though it does not actually yield theoretical knowledge. Morality with its cosmological presuppositions gives a further dimension of completeness to our view of self and world which theoretical reason strives towards but cannot itself demonstrate. It is for this reason, I would suggest, that Kant sees morality as extending theoretical reason.[35]

I have, then, shown both why Kant would feel justified in reserving the term sublime exclusively for moral consciousness, and why even theoretical reason falls victim to this exclusion. Both these points will prove important to our understanding of the theory of the sublime outlined in the *Critique of Judgement*.

In conclusion, therefore, it is clear that Kant's attitude to the sublime in his Critical ethics is one that serves to locate it wholly beyond the artistic and aesthetic sphere. However, in the

---

[35] See e.g. his arguments in *Practical Reason*, 236–7.

Critique of Judgement he offers us a theory which attempts to bridge the gap between sublimity as a moral and as an aesthetic concept. To understand this bridging we must first grasp the essentials of the overall aesthetic theory proposed in the third *Critique*. It is to this task I now turn.

PART II

The Aesthetics of the Sublime

3

Kant's Aesthetic Theory and its Moral Significance

The *Critique of Judgement* divides fundamentally into three parts—the Introduction, the Critique of Aesthetic Judgement, and the Critique of Teleological Judgement. In this chapter I will be concentrating primarily on the salient aspects of the first two of these.

I

Kant's main arguments in the Introduction begin with Section II. They are somewhat difficult to follow, but hinge on the following points. Understanding, with its pure concepts of nature, legislates what form the phenomenal world will take. Reason, in contrast, legislates for our practical vocation as autonomous supersensible beings. Now, while in the phenomenal world the effects of these legislative powers can modify one another (e.g. our moral decisions can override our sensible inclinations), such powers are, *qua* legislative, logically independent of one another. As Kant puts it, a 'great gulf' exists between them. However,

the concept of freedom is meant to actualise in the sensible world the end proposed by its laws; and nature must consequently also be capable of being regarded in such a way that in the conformity to law of its form it at least harmonises with the possibility of the ends to be effectuated in it according to the laws of freedom.[1]

But why must nature be capable of being thought of as ordered in harmony with the realization of our moral ends? Kant's answer to this is, in effect, a continuation and completion of the thesis concerning the absolute primacy of practical reason (discussed in the preceding chapter of this study). For example, in Section IX

[1] Kant, *Judgement*, Part I, p. 14.

of the Introduction, we are told that the effect of the concept of freedom 'is the final end which (or the manifestation of which in the sensible world) is to exist, and this presupposes the condition of the posssibility of that end in nature'.[2]

To understand this passage, it is worth pointing out first that for Kant something counts as an 'end' if it is a concept which can be thought of as the causal ground of some object's actuality.[3] This means specifically that the object's existence can only be explained or made intelligible through an analogy with artifice, that is by viewing as if it had been produced in order to realize some end or function willed by the artificer. The meaning of the term *final end* only receives an adequate clarification in § 25 of the Critique of Teleological Judgement. There Kant informs us that

all the manifold forms of life, co-ordinated though they may be with the greatest art and concatenated with the utmost variety of final adaptations, and even the entire complex that embraces their numerous systems . . . would all exist for nothing, if man or other rational beings of some sort were not found in their midst. Without man, in other words, the whole of creation would be a mere wilderness, a thing in vain, and have no final end.[4]

Given that for Kant the phenomenal world's most fundamental structural features arise from the combined function of the forms of intuition and the categories (i.e. presuppose the human subject), the very idea of a world without humans in its midst may seem at least odd or at worst contradictory. One supposes, however, that some other life-form possessed of a rudimentary sensibility and understanding, but lacking the capacity to think and act on the basis of its own idea of principles (i.e. reason), *could* also have constituted a phenomenal world roughly similar to our own. The idea of a world without human beings, in other words, is at least logically possible, but it is not rationally acceptable to Kant. For if we did not regard the world as created with the needs of rational beings in view (i.e. with man as its 'final end') it would be devoid of worth. This would mean (in effect) that we could offer no explanation as to why it existed at

---

[2] Kant, *Judgement*, Part I, p. 38.
[3] See e.g. the definition in Section IV of the Introduction (ibid. 19). Cf. also ibid. § 10, p. 61.
[4] Ibid. Part II, p. 108.

all—and such a dimension of contingency (for Kant at least) would be contrary to reason's demand for the unconditional in knowledge. Now while to avoid such unacceptable contingency we must necessarily assume that rational beings such as ourselves are the final end of creation, it is, nevertheless, not man in his role as an executant of theoretical reason who gives the world its *raison d'être*. For

> if this contemplation of the world brought to light nothing but things without a final end, the existence of the world could not acquire a worth from being known. A final end of the world must be presupposed as that in relation to which the contemplation of the world may itself possess a worth.[5]

This ultimate point of reference is provided by man in his moral being. As Kant puts it, 'a good will is that whereby man's existence alone can possess an absolute worth, and in relation to which the existence of the world can have a final end'.[6]

Hitherto in the Critical philosophy, Kant has presented nature (at least in the form of our sensuous impulses) as wholly antagonistic to morality. The feeling of respect is the one exception to this, but even here feeling only proves conducive to morality through it being the effect of the moral law's humiliation of our natural being and its aspirations. However, given that in the third *Critique* Kant is now prepared to declare that our moral vocation must be assumed to be the final end or *raison d'être* of *all* existence (including, one presumes, nature), it would be unacceptable for the natural domain to be regarded as wholly antagonistic or indifferent to morality. We must assume rather that (while remaining logically independent of the grounds of morality) nature is in some sense in 'harmony' with our moral vocation (i.e. is capable of promoting it *indirectly*).

Now the question arises as to what form this harmony takes. In the Introduction Kant remarks that the 'condition of the possibility' of the final end in nature is to be found 'in the nature of the Subject as a being of the sensible world, namely as man'.[7] On these terms, if morality is in some way to be indirectly promoted by nature, it could only be so through some aspect of humanity's natural or sensible being. One presumes that the

---

[5] Ibid. Part II, p. 108.   [6] Ibid. Part II, p. 109.
[7] Ibid. Part I, p. 38.

reason for this is (as is clear from the foregoing passages in the Critique of Teleological Judgement) that nature considered without reference to humanity is, so to speak, axiologically inert—a mere 'wilderness'. It could, accordingly, only be the natural world as related to, or manifest in, some aspect of human sensibility which marks the positive[8] bridging point between brute nature and supersensible freedom. This opens up two possibilities. First, nature's indirect promotion of morality may pertain to the way in which we order the former according to subjective theoretical principles 'in' us; and second, it may pertain to some aspect of our affective being—such as feeling. In practice, as I shall now argue, Kant links nature to freedom on the basis of both these approaches.

The clue which enables Kant to begin this task is provided by a gap in the overall Critical architectonic. For Kant, judgement in general is a psychological power which enables the understanding's concepts or 'rules' to be brought to bear on the imagination's manifold of sensible intuitions, in a way that confers unity on that manifold. In terms of the Critical architectonics, this (though Kant does not say why) places judgement between Understanding and Reason in the faculty of cognition, and, indeed, parallels a similar intermediate placing of the feeling of pleasure and pain between cognition and desire in the 'faculties of the soul' generally. Kant proposes, therefore, that if an a priori principle can be found for judgement (as similar principles were found for Understanding and Reason in the first two *Critiques*) then this will relate to the feeling of pleasure or pain (a faculty 'necessarily combined' with that of desire) in a way which 'will effect a transition from the faculty of pure knowledge, i.e. from the realm of concepts of nature, to that of the concept of freedom'.[9]

The best way of understanding Kant's reasoning here is to see how he puts it into practice. We must start from Section IV of the Introduction, where a fundamental distinction is made between 'determinant' and 'reflective' judgements on the basis of the kind of concepts that each employ. The former involve those pure concepts of understanding (the 'categories') which are

[8] Respect, of course, is only a negative bridging point—a humiliation of our natural being.

[9] *Judgement*, 17.

presupposed by any experience; the latter involve finding concepts for particular empirical objects. Kant, however, complicates this rather straightforward distinction between the a priori and empirical employment of judgement in the following way. While the application of the categories establishes objectivity in our experience of nature, this does not of itself entail that finite intellects such as ours will be able to grasp the multiplicity of individual empirical laws of nature and their interrelations as a systematic totality. Understanding could cope with this empirical multiplicity to some degree in a piecemeal way by forming aggregates of knowledge. But, as we saw in Chapter 2, for Kant the 'interest' of theoretical reason strives towards complete and unconditionally systematic knowledge. Hence he is led to suppose that in relation to nature's potentially overwhelming empirical diversity the reflective judgement is guided by an a priori regulative principle of its own—namely the assumption that nature is 'final' in relation to the 'end' of human cognition.[10] To understand this principle of 'finality' we must first recall that for Kant an 'end' is a concept which (on the basis of an analogy with artifice) is regarded as the ground of an object's existence. Hence the a priori principle of reflective judgement regards nature *as if* its form had been designed by some artificer, with the express end of facilitating human cognition. This means specifically that we assume nature to be ordered in terms of a hierarchical continuity of ends. For example, in judging a particular rose we will treat the flower *as if* it had been designed with the end of instantiating that set of properties which define the rose as a natural kind. We will regard the particular flower as 'final' in relation to the 'end' *rosehood*. More generally, Kant suggests that

There is in nature a subordination of genera and species comprehensible by us. Each of these genera again approximates to the others on a common principle, so that a transition may be possible from one to another, and thereby to a higher genus.[11]

---

[10] Being final in relation to an end is not the same thing as the 'final end' noted earlier. The latter term pertains to the assumed *raison d'être* of all existence, whereas the former concerns that which is assumed in relation to the existence of particular instances of natural kinds.

[11] *Judgement*, 24.

This principle of natural finality constitutes, in effect, the first step in Kant's bridging of the 'gulf' between nature and freedom. As he puts it in the Critique of Teleological Judgement,

without man the chain of mutually subordinated ends would have no ultimate point of attachment. Only in man, and only in him as the individual to whom the moral law applies, do we find unconditional legislation in respect of ends. This legislation, therefore, is what alone qualifies him to be a final end to which entire nature is teleologically subordinated.[12]

On these terms, if we regard nature theoretically as a hierarchical system of ends, we will be led ultimately to a final end which is the *raison d'être* of the whole system. This means that we will arrive at the notion of the free rational being. Now while this transition of thought bridges the gulf between nature and freedom at the level of the higher cognitive faculties, Kant must also (in order completely to fill the architectonic gap noted earlier) show how a similar bridging is brought about by the relation between finality (as a subjective principle of cognition) and the feeling of pleasure and pain, in the context of the 'faculties of the soul' in general. This second step begins with Section IV—'The Association of the Feeling of Pleasure with the Concept of the Finality of Nature'. It proves, unfortunately, to be one of the most confused sections in the whole of the third *Critique*, and requires both detailed exposition and reformulation before we can discern Kant's underlying strategy.

The first major point of substance involves the claim that

The attainment of every aim is coupled with a feeling of pleasure. Now where such cognition has for its condition a representation *a priori*—as here a principle for the reflective judgement in general—the feeling of pleasure is determined by a ground which is *a priori* and valid for all men; and that too, merely by reference of the Object to our faculty of cognition.[13]

Such pleasure (Kant continues) does not arise from the determinant judgement since in this case 'understanding necessarily follows the bent of its own nature without ulterior aim'.[14] He then illustrates the contrast at issue here by way of an example:

---

[12] *Judgement*, Part II, § 23, pp. 99–100.
[13] Ibid. Part I, p. 27.   [14] Ibid. 27.

the discovery, on the other hand, that two or more empirical heterogeneous laws of nature are allied under one principle that embraces them both, is the ground of a very appreciable pleasure . . . as does not wear off when we are already familiar enough with its object.[15]

It is, in other words, the reflective judgement whose a priori determining principle can be the source of pleasure. Kant's reasoning in these passages is based on the fact that, while the aim of cognition in general is the attainment of knowledge, the knowledge which arises from determinative judgements (through their employment of the categories) is *constitutive*. If such judgements were not always successful, there would be no experience of any sort. Given the necessary guarantee of success, it makes no sense to regard such judgements as attaining or achieving the aim of knowledge. In the case of reflective judgements, however, the a priori principle which informs them is *regulative* only. In order to achieve systematic knowledge of nature's empirical diversity we have to regard nature *as if* it were teleologically ordered. But this provides no guarantee that (as it were) the particular piece of empirical diversity we are attending to will be immediately graspable in terms of a specific teleological principle. Here the a priori principle allows for the possibility of both success and failure in the judgements which apply it. It is meaningful, therefore, to regard successful judgements of this sort as attaining the aim of cognition. Now even if we allow Kant's claim that the reflective judgement involves the pleasure-inducing 'attainment' of an 'aim', other serious problems still arise. For example, in Section VIII, we are told that the reflective judgement of 'logical finality' which 'refers the form of the Object, not to the Subject's cognitive faculties engaged in its apprehension, but to a definite object under a given concept, has *nothing to do with a feeling of pleasure in things*' (my italics).[16] Given the fact that Kant's example in Section VII of the subsumption of two empirical laws under a higher principle quite clearly involves definite objects being brought under a concept, it surely follows that it is an example of the pleasure-indifferent judgement of logical finality. Matters are further complicated by the fact that, having attributed a 'very appreciable pleasure' that 'does not wear off' through familiarity with its object to an

---

[15] Ibid. 27.   [16] Ibid. 33–4.

example of such a judgement, Kant immediately goes on to declare that

> It is true that we no longer notice any decided pleasure in the comprehensibility of nature, or in the unity of its divisions into genera and species . . . Still it is certain that the pleasure appeared in due course, and only by reason of the most ordinary experience being impossible without it, has it become gradually fused with simple cognition, and no longer arrests particular attention.[17]

As well as contradicting the statements which precede it, this passage's claim that the 'most ordinary experience' is 'impossible' without a certain mode of pleasure is, to say the least, wildly at odds with his general Critical epistemology. These logical difficulties can be avoided (in a way that clarifies the underlying thrust of Kant's argument) by modifying and restating his position in terms of the following series of points. (i) Unlike determinative judgements, all successful reflective judgements of finality involve the attainment of an aim. (ii) Since the attainment of every aim is coupled with a feeling of pleasure, it follows that every successful reflective judgement of finality will be so accompanied. (iii) This can be illustrated by the fact that we take pleasure in the discovery that two particular empirical laws of nature can be subsumed under a higher principle. (iv) However, while this example brings out the desired contrast with determinative judgements, it must be regarded as exceptional. (v) The reason for this is that, even though such reflective judgements of logical finality are not constitutive of experience, they are nevertheless so familiar and of such great utility in the theoretical domain as to make it almost impossible to imagine ordinary day-to-day experience without them. (As Kant puts it in Section VIII, without such judgements of finality 'understanding could not feel itself at home in nature'.[18]) (vi) Hence, one might say that it is the very familiarity and (in a sense) *inescapability* of judgements of logical finality which serve wholly to distract us from the pleasure which, when successful, they necessarily give rise to. (vii) This is why the example noted in (iii) must be regarded as exceptional, and why, generally speaking, judgements of logical finality *seem* to have nothing to do with pleasure at all.

[17] *Judgement*, Part II, § 22, pp. 27–8.   [18] *Judgement*, 35.

Restating Kant's argument in this consistent form (and overlooking any further interpretative and critical issues it raises) brings us to a crucial point of transition. We are told that

Something, then, that makes us attentive in our estimate of nature to its finality for our understanding . . . is required in order that, on meeting with success, pleasure may be felt in this . . . accord [of nature's empirical laws] with our cognitive faculty . . .[19]

We require something that draws attention to the finality of nature in a way that will make us *conscious* of our pleasure in judgements that successfully put such a principle into practice. We need, in effect, a special form of reflective judgement. But why is it required that such pleasure be felt rather than pass unnoticed? What is its significance? The answer to this is only manifest when Kant has outlined that special form of reflective judgement—namely the aesthetic—wherein our pleasure in natural finality is enjoyed explicitly. I shall consider the structure of such judgements at length in a few moments. For the present it is sufficient to note that, if (irrespective of a knowledge of what kind of thing it is, or of what use it serves) some object engages the cognitive faculties in a way that brings them into especially harmonious and playful co-operation, then such an object is final in relation to the end of cognition generally. This harmony is only recognizable through the feeling of pleasure it engenders. Kant then makes his decisive claim—

The spontaneity in the play of the cognitive faculties whose harmonious accord contains the ground of this pleasure, makes the concept in question [i.e. of the finality of nature] in its consequences, a suitable mediating link connecting the concept of nature with that of the concept of freedom, as this accord at the same time promotes the sensibility of the mind for moral feeling.[20]

The reason why it is so important that our pleasure in successful reflective judgements should actually be felt is that it arises from an accord of the faculties which is conducive to moral feeling. This invites two closely related questions. First, why is it that (in contrast with logical finality) our pleasure in aesthetic judgements *is* felt so explicitly, and, second, why is it that the accord of the faculties which gives rise to this explicit pleasure is

[19] Ibid. 28.   [20] Ibid. 39.

one which also disposes us to moral feeling? In relation to the first
of these, one might answer the question by way of a contrast. In
the case of judgements of logical finality two levels of significance
are involved. On the one hand, as instances of the type 'reflective
judgement' they are informed by the principle that nature is final
in relation to the end of cognition. Hence, when we judge an
object as final in relation to some end or other, this successful
employment of the principle gives rise to a feeling of pleasure. On
the other hand, *qua* logical judgements, the particular way in
which they embody this principle of finality is by referring the
object to some definite concept of an end. It is this logical
function which makes them so familiar and widely employed—so
much so that our pleasure in them passes unnoticed. In the case
of the aesthetic judgement, we have the first pleasure-arousing
level of significance, but not the second level with its distracting
features. It follows that in this case the reflective judgement is
found more consciously pleasurable. This contrast also points
toward the link with morality. For while the judgement of logical
finality is restricted (and, as it were, rendered impure) by
reference to a definite concept of an end, in the pure aesthetic
judgement there is no such empirical constraint. Here our
pleasure arises solely from the harmony of the faculties achieved
through their accord with the mere form of an object, on the basis
of an a priori principle. In this latter case, therefore, our
pleasure is grounded more purely in the a priori (and thence
supersensible) domain than is the case with judgements of logical
finality. As Kant puts it in the first version of the Introduction to
the third *Critique*, the pure aesthetic judgement is characterized
by its 'heautonomy', that is, has something in common with the
a priori autonomy which accrues to moral principles.[21] To
experience aesthetic pleasure, in consequence, is to have one's
capacity for feeling determined in a mode analogous to the
effect of morality upon feeling. Kant seems to suppose that

---

[21] Kant, *First Introduction to the Critique of Judgement*, trans. James Haden
(Bobbs Merrill: New York, 1965), 29. Kant uses the term 'heautonomy' because,
while the reflective judgement is guided by its own a priori principle, it is not
constitutive for the objects it is directed towards (i.e. nature). Understanding and
practical reason, in contrast, are objectively 'autonomous' because not only do they
have their own a priori principles, but these are indeed constitutive of their respective
objects—namely nature and freedom. Cf. also Section V in the official version of the
Introduction to the third *Critique* (op. cit. p. 25).

susceptibility to aesthetic pleasure will also tend to make us susceptible to moral feeling. I shall defer a fuller discussion of the issues involved here until Section III of this chapter.

To summarize, then. (i) In the third *Critique*, Kant holds that our moral vocation with its laws of freedom must be assumed to be the final end of all creation. (ii) This means, in turn, that we must assume nature to be ordered in such a way as indirectly to promote moral ends. (iii) This 'harmony' arises from the employment of an a priori principle of finality, which mediates between understanding and reason in the higher faculties of cognition, and also serves to determine that feeling of pleasure or pain which is mediately placed between cognition and desire in the faculties of the soul generally. (iv) More specifically, Kant shows that in its former function the principle of finality leads us from nature construed as a teleological system, to freedom construed as its final end; and in its latter function gives rise to a mode of feeling that in turn makes us susceptible to moral feeling.

The first of these morally significant functions is largely explored in the Appendix to the Critique of Teleological Judgement; the second is considered mainly in the Critique of Aesthetic Judgement. It is to this latter work I now turn.

II

The fundamentals of Kant's aesthetic theory are provided in Part I of the Critique of Aesthetic Judgement—entitled the Analytic of the Beautiful. It is subdivided into four 'Moments' which each consider the aesthetic judgement from a different aspect. These are: (i) qualitative, (ii) quantitative, (iii) relational, and (iv) modal. Moments (iii) and (i) concern the grounds of aesthetic judgement, and (ii) and (iv) concern the judgement's epistemological status. In relation to the grounds of the aesthetic judgement, Kant's arguments are somewhat unwieldy and are best approached by tracing and developing material from both the Introduction and the relevant Moments. Consideration of Kant's arguments concerning the epistemological status of aesthetic judgements, in contrast, is best focused on an analysis of Moments (ii) and (iv) in sequence (a task which I will address in the next section of this chapter).

First, then, the grounds of the aesthetic judgement. Kant's position on this issue arises, one might say, from the conjunction of two dimensions of subjectivity. The first of these is outlined at the very start of the Analytic of the Beautiful, where Kant defines the aesthetic judgement as one whose determining ground is wholly subjective. Such a judgement 'denotes nothing in the object, but is a feeling which the Subject has of itself and of the manner in which it is affected by the representation'.[22]

For example, the 'material' aesthetic judgement arises from an empirically knowable (or, as Kant sometimes describes it, 'pathological'[23]) relation. Hence, in saying 'this wine is very agreeable' the predicate of our judgement expresses a subjective effect of the object, rather than an objective cognition of it. But aesthetic *reflective* judgements (briefly outlined in Section I of this chapter) are rather more complex. To understand how pleasure arises from these, it is first useful to look briefly at the transcendental synthesis of imagination which Kant outlines in the first edition[24] of the *Critique of Pure Reason*. This has a threefold structure, (*a*) in the 'synthesis of apprehension' the manifold of sensible intuitions is 'run through and held together',[25] that is, the parts of the manifold must be individuated successively in time. However,

even this apprehension of the manifold would not by itself produce an image and a connection of the impressions, were it not that there exists a subjective ground which leads the mind to reinstate a preceding perception alongside the subsequent perception to which it has passed, and so to form whole series of perceptions.[26]

---

[22] *Judgement*, Book I, § 1, p. 42.

[23] Cf. Kant, *Pure Reason*, A802/B830, p. 633.

[24] Reference to the first edition is more appropriate here because, while the second edition's version of the transcendental synthesis is generally considered to be philosophically superior, it is, nevertheless, the first edition's account which more closely corresponds to the approach taken in the third *Critique*. In this respect, for example, one might cite Kant's pairing of apprehension and aesthetic comprehension in § 26 of the Analytic of the Sublime—which directly parallels the syntheses of imagination and reproduction in the *Critique of Pure Reason*'s first edition. Indeed, the general emphasis which Kant places on transcendental psychology in the first edition of the first *Critique* deeply complements the Critique of Aesthetic Judgement's focusing on the 'subjective' conditions of cognition.

[25] *Pure Reason*, A99, p. 131.   [26] Ibid. A121, p. 144.

This 'subjective ground' Kant terms (*b*) the 'synthesis of reproduction in imagination'. Yet even this is not yet sufficient to unite the manifold. The reproductive capacity which sustains apprehension must 'conform to a rule, in accordance with which a representation connects in the imagination with some one representation in preference to another'.[27]

This conformity to a rule Kant calls (*c*) 'the synthesis of recognition in a concept'. There are two things to note about this threefold synthesis. First, it consists essentially in the temporalization of concepts, that is, imagination through (*a*) and (*b*) provides the conditions whereby concepts can determine 'inner sense'—Kant's term for time. (This process Kant also describes as 'schematization'.) Second, to the modern philosopher (*a*), (*b*), and (*c*) sound like the mutually implicatory logical conditions of any experience, but while, for Kant, the term 'transcendental' carries similar connotations, it also has a crucial *psychological* dimension. For him, (*a*), (*b*), and (*c*) constitute 'acts of mind' and, for any cognition to be subjectively possible, (*a*) and (*b*) (involving the faculty of imagination) must co-operate at the psychological level (i.e. be in 'harmony') with (*c*) (the faculty of understanding).

For Kant, it is to this subjective psychological harmony of the faculties that we must look in order to find the ground of our pleasure in the aesthetic reflective judgement (hereafter referred to as the judgement of taste). Kant summarizes the process involved as follows:

If pleasure is connected with the mere apprehension . . . of the form of an object of intuition, apart from any reference it may have to a concept, for the purpose of a definite cognition, this does not make the representation referable to the Object, but solely to the Subject. In such a case, the pleasure can express nothing but the conformity of the Object to the cognitive faculties brought into play in the reflective judgement.[28]

On these terms, in the judgement of taste an object engages the faculties of cognition in a harmonious relationship which does not, as in the logical reflective judgement, issue in us recognizing the object as final in relation to some specific empirical concept of an end. Instead there is something about the form of the object which stimulates imagination and understanding into an

---

[27] Ibid. A121, p. 144. [28] *Judgement*, Part I, p. 30.

unusually lively or 'free' co-operation. Since the very function or 'end' of imagination and understanding is to co-operate with one another so as to achieve knowledge of objects, the fact that the judgement of taste stimulates this co-operation to a heightened degree means that it is final in relation to cognition generally. By harmonizing the interaction of the faculties at the subjective level, the form of the object successfully exemplifies the a priori assumption that nature is so adapted as to facilitate the task of cognition. It must, however, be noted (even though Kant himself sometimes seems to suggest otherwise[29]) that this exemplification does not involve an explicit appraisal to the effect 'this object's form is final in relation to cognition generally'. Rather the harmony of the faculties achieved through our judgement of taste is recognized only by the feeling of pleasure it gives rise to.

This provisional presentation of Kant's theory raises two major questions. First, what is it about the form of the object which stimulates this harmony; and second, given that the transcendental synthesis of imagination (noted earlier) is both presupposed by any experience and *involves 'recognition in a concept'*, how can Kant now assert that there is a mode of judgement recognizable only through a feeling of pleasure? In relation to the first of these questions Kant remarks in the Third Moment that 'Beauty is the form of finality in an object, so far as perceived in it apart from an end.'[30]

---

[29] See e.g. Kant's remark at the end of the Analytic of the Beautiful to the effect that taste is 'a critical faculty by which an object is estimated in reference to the *free conformity to law* of the imagination' (ibid. 85). The fact that Kant adopts a tone here which suggests explicit appraisals on the basis of definite concepts is to be explained by the fact that, while the beautiful is only consciously recognized through the pleasure we feel in it, the fact that we have such pleasure at all can only be explained (as I shall elucidate a little further on) through its being grounded in *cognitive activity* of such complexity as to elude being grasped in any definite concept. Kant is trying to emphasize that, while being aesthetic, our pleasure in beauty is dissimilar from that of mere charm or agreeableness. Conversely, when Kant wishes to stress the judgement of taste's dissimilarity to those that involve definite concepts of the object (e.g. ones which pertain to logical finality or the good) he sometimes expresses himself in terms which suggest that feeling alone is involved. For example, in § 5 we are told that the judgement of taste is not 'a cognitive judgement' and 'only decides how its [i.e. the object's] character stands with the feeling of pleasure or displeasure' (ibid. 48).

[30] Ibid. 80. It is striking that, while earlier on in the third *Critique* (ibid. § 6, 51) Kant suggests that the judgement of taste only predicates beauty *as if* it were an objective property of the object, his phrasing here suggests that beauty *is* a property of the object. The most that Kant can legitimately claim, however, is that, although our pleasure in the object arises from the way in which it harmonizes the faculties, it

Now 'form of finality' here is not the same notion as that 'finality of form' (discussed earlier) which an object has in relation to its concept of an end. It is a term (along with its synonyms 'formal finality'[31] and 'subjective finality') which Kant uses both to denote those formal configurations which have an appearance of purposiveness or design—yet without being final in relation to any definite empirical end—and also to pick out the 'free' harmony of the faculties achieved through our cognition of such forms. By considering the relation between these two notions in detail here we shall be able to answer both the questions noted above. A good starting-point is Kant's observation in § 35 that

since the freedom of imagination consists precisely in the fact that it schematizes without a concept, the judgement of taste must rest upon a mere sensation of the mutually quickening activity of the imagination in its freedom, and of the understanding in its conformity to law.[32]

At face value, the first part of this statement seems nonsensical in so far as (according to the *Critique of Pure Reason*) to schematize simply *is* a case of the imagination providing temporal conditions whereby a concept can be applied to intuition. It should also be remembered from the first *Critique* that no experience is possible at all without the application of the pure concepts of understanding. However, while Kant suggests that free imagination schematizes without *a* concept, he does not mean that it schematizes without reference to the *faculty* of concepts as such. One might illustrate this as follows. Suppose that we are attending to a complex of intertwining foliage. To experience such foliage at all entails that we must be able to grasp it in terms of some concept or other.[33] But if we consider the foliage as a

would not be able to do so if its manifold did not have an objective structure of the requisite complexity. On these terms Kant would express himself more appropriately by saying that beauty is a function of the relation between the objective characteristics of a manifold and the cognitive faculties of the subject.

[31] Kant (characteristically) complicates his terminology by occasionally using 'formal finality' and 'subjective finality' in a somewhat broader sense to emphasize the fact that the principle of teleological classification is subjectively grounded, i.e. not a constitutive feature of experience, in the way, for example, that the categories are. (Cf. Introduction, Section VIII, ibid. 34.)

[32] Ibid. 143.

[33] Cf. General Remark on the First Section of the Analytic, ibid. 86.

formal configuration alone (i.e. as a complex of shape, colour, mass, density, line, etc.), the way in which our attention is engaged may, cognitively speaking, be too rich and complex to be characterized simply in terms of the single concept 'intertwining foliage'. We might contemplate it through successive moments tracing the overall contours and balance of its structure in different directions. We might attend to specific textural details, noting their relationship to one another and to the complex as a whole. Indeed the more possibilities of perceptually exploring the relation between parts and whole emerge, the more the imagination is free to prolong attention and store up images of the complex. Reciprocally, the more we are inclined to apprehend the foliage through time, the more it is likely that further new ways of understanding its phenomenal structure will appear. In this case, imagination and understanding are in a particularly harmonious accord. The former functions as 'an originator of arbitrary forms of possible intuitions'.[34] This means, in effect, that it presents understanding with a multiplicity of possible ways of unifying a manifold of sensible intuition—so much so that it is best characterized as engaging our capacity for conceptualizing (i.e. 'faculty of concepts' as such rather than any one concept in particular).[35] On these terms, while an object considered in purely formal terms has unity, it is a unity which can be synthesized in a number of different ways. Given this, one might say that the object will have the appearance of finality in so far as the complex cognitive engagement it gives rise to serves to harmonize the faculties and thus promotes the end of cognition generally. Yet because this engagement is so psychologically complex we will not explicitly recognize the object as final in relation to this or any other definite end. Rather the judgement of taste will strike us fundamentally in terms of the pleasure which arises from its complex causal ground.

Even if we allow this presentation of Kant's position, Paul Guyer has questioned the privileged role he assigns here to formal qualities. As Guyer puts it,

the only purpose which beautiful objects can appear designed to fulfill without being actually judged to be designed is the general purpose of cognition itself. But unless we have already placed some constraints on

---

[34] *Judgement*, 86.   [35] Cf. ibid. §9, p. 58.

the features by which objects can produce the harmony of the faculties, their appearing designed for this purpose can imply no such restraints.[36]

However, in so far as the harmony requisite to the purpose of cognition is between the faculties of imagination and understanding, and does not involve reference to sensibility or desire, this, of itself, implies some rather severe constraints on what will contribute to subjective finality. What these constraints are becomes clearer through Kant's notion of disinterestedness outlined in the First Moment. He tells us, for example, that

The delight which we connect with the representation of the real existence of an object is called interest. Such a delight, therefore, always involves a reference to the faculty of desire, either as its determining ground, or else as necessarily implicated with its determining ground.[37]

The relationship of interest to desire is clarified in § 3 and § 4 of the Analytic of the Beautiful, which deal with the agreeable and the good respectively. In relation to the former, Kant suggests that to predicate agreeableness of an object expresses an interest in it, inasmuch as it provokes a desire for other objects of the same kind. Similarly, in relation to the good and useful, we are told that 'In both cases the concept of an end is implied, and consequently the relation of reason to (an at least possible) willing, and thus a delight in the *existence* of an Object of action, i.e. some interest or other.'[38] What I take Kant to mean by all these points is that, if an object or action is a source of delight, then it is the kind of thing that we would desire or will to have real existence, even if it did not. It is interesting in this respect that Kant often talks of our delight in 'real existence' rather than 'existence' alone. By this emphasis, he can be taken to mean that, if we desire that something exists, we are not simply delighted by the *appearance* that it exists. For example, if, having tasted a quail's egg, we desire more of the same, a hollow shell will not satisfy us. Similarly, if we delight in goodness, the appearance of a moral action will not please us, unless we have grounds for believing that it was performed for the right sort of motive. In

---

[36] Paul Guyer, *Kant and the Claims of Taste* (Harvard University Press: London and Cambridge, Mass., 1981), 221–2.

[37] *Judgement*, § 2, p. 42.   [38] Ibid. 46.

these cases we desire not just the appearance of the object or action (i.e. its phenomenal qualities), but also those unapparent but necessary qualities which would constitute the reality of its existence.

For Kant, then, an interest entails delighting in, and thereby desiring, the real existence of its object. These points now enable us to rectify a mistake made by Guyer. He suggests that

> In § 3, Kant differentiates pleasure in a beautiful object from that in an agreeable one by claiming that the latter produces an interest in further experiences of the same sort, and implying that the former does not. However, it appears to be a defining characteristic of any kind of pleaure that it produce an interest in its own continuation, and this makes the difference between the beautiful and agreeable obscure indeed.[39]

Now Kant does state that *any* pleasure will tend towards self-prolongation, and Guyer is right, therefore, to suggest that this will not clarify the difference between the agreeable and the beautiful. However, given Kant's technical usage (noted above) Guyer is wrong in describing this tendency as an 'interest'. Indeed it is by overlooking this technical sense that Guyer is led, in the first sentence of the quotation, to overlook the grounds on which Kant *does* separate the agreeable and the beautiful. In the relevant passage[40] Kant states that the agreeable provokes a desire not (as Guyer says) for similar experiences, but, rather, for similar *objects* which will provide such experiences. Since a mere appearance could not provide these, what we desire here is an object with real, rather than apparent, existence. This, as I pointed out above, is also true of our interest in the good. To delight in the beautiful, in contrast, is wholly disinterested, and does not stimulate a desire for the real object, because our pleasure arises from the contemplation of form alone. From the viewpoint of beauty, illusory or dreamed intertwining foliage will serve just as well as the real thing. What the object is, empirically speaking, or what its exact ontological status is, have in themselves no bearing on us finding them beautiful. This is why Kant further differentiates the good and the beautiful on the grounds that

> To deem something good, I must always know what sort of thing it is intended to be, i.e. I must have a concept of it. That is not necessary to

[39] Guyer, op. cit. (n. 36 above), 182.   [40] *Judgement*, 45.

enable me to see beauty in a thing. Flowers, free patterns, lines aimlessly intertwining—technically termed foliage [!],—have no signification, depend on no definite concept, and yet please.[41]

We find that Kant's understanding of interest and disinterested reinforces and extends the basic point entailed by the thesis of the harmony of imagination and understanding—that the ground of our pleasure in the beautiful (subjective finality) extends only to formal elements of phenomenal structure. In Kant's technical usage, even the imagination imports no sensuous element into subjective finality, concerned as it is with the merely temporal ordering of the manifold of sensible intuition. This approach is taken to a somewhat implausible extreme in the Third Moment, where Kant completes his account of subjective finality by a total separation of it from any element of agreeable sensation. As he puts it,

In painting, sculpture, and in fact all the formative arts, in architecture and horticulture, so far as fine arts, the *design* is what is essential. Here it is not what gratifies in sensation but merely what pleases by its form, that is the fundamental prerequisite for taste. The colours which give brilliance to the sketch are part of the charm. They may no doubt, in their own way, enliven the object for sensation, but make it really worth looking at and beautiful they cannot.[42]

Let me now summarize the major points in this section. (i) Judgements of taste are a special form of reflective judgement wherein the subjective conditions of cognition (imagination and understanding) are in a harmonious accord which is conducive to cognition generally. (ii) The psychological complexity of such judgements means that this harmony of the faculties can only be recognized by the feeling of pleasure it gives rise to. (iii) Such a harmony is brought about by our judging an object strictly in terms of its formal qualities. Specifically, this involves the object having the 'form of finality', that is, an appearance of design which is able (even though we are not explicitly conscious of the fact) to stimulate the co-operation of the faculties in a way that promotes the end of cognition generally. (iv) The pleasure which is generated from such origins is wholly disinterested in relation to the 'real existence' of the object.

[41] Ibid. 46.   [42] Ibid. 67.

Kant's arguments raise many critical and interpretative issues other than the ones I have touched upon in my exposition and notes. I shall overlook these on the grounds that in Chapter 6 I shall be restating a version of Kant's theory which is free from the difficulties imposed by technical notions (such as the reflective judgement, and the doctrine of the faculties). For present purposes, it suffices to point out that the fundamental strategy of Kant's explanation of the grounds of the judgement of taste in the Introduction and Analytic of the Beautiful is to establish it on an a priori rather than empirical basis. This not only presents the judgement of taste as a logically distinct mode of experience, but also clears the way for an ultimate linking of it with morality. It is, however (as I shall now show), in the context of the epistemological status of judgements of taste that this link is actually made.

III

The central epistemological task of the third *Critique* is to establish that judgements of taste possess synthetic a priori validity. That such judgements are synthetic is easily demonstrable, in so far as the predicate 'beautiful' asserts a feeling we enjoy in relation to an object, rather than a property logically 'contained' in the concept of the object. But this illustrates the fundamental problem of the judgement of taste, namely how can an assertion of our subjective response lay claim to a priori, as opposed to merely private, validity? The Deduction by which Kant attempts to solve this problem is, in effect, spread out over three separate sections of the third *Critique*. I shall now consider these in turn.

First, in the Analytic of the Beautiful (Second Moment) Kant claims that 'The beautiful is that which, apart from concepts, is represented as the Object of a UNIVERSAL delight.'[43] Kant then proceeds to utilize points established in the First Moment. Given that our pleasure in the beautiful is disinterested, this clearly points to a foundation other than that of the agreeable or good. Now ordinary usage of the term 'beautiful' also suggests that our disinterested pleasure is universally valid, in the

[43] *Judgement*, 50.

sense of commanding the agreement of everyone. However, where ordinary usage overreaches itself is in supposing that this universal validity arises from the role of concepts. Kant holds that this cannot be so, because a pleasure which logically presupposes some concept of the object entails an interest in its real existence. It is not, in other words, disinterested. In what, then, *does* universality of the judgement of taste consist? Kant's strategy is as follows. The ground of our pleasure in the beautiful must be, if not objective, then at least 'universally communicable' (i.e. intersubjectively valid). The only aspects of experience which are universally communicable are those which pertain to cognition; but, as we have just seen, the universal communicability to be drawn upon here cannot be that of concepts. This means that if the judgement of taste is to have intersubjective validity, we must look for its ground in the subjective conditions of cognition—namely that psychological harmony of the faculties discussed earlier in this chapter.

Kant does not, in the Second Moment, develop the Deduction beyond these very general terms. In the Fourth Moment, though, he does take up the thread again—initially by reformulating the question which the Deduction is to answer, in strictly modal terms. His procedure is as follows. We feel that our pleasure in the beautiful has some claim to *necessity*. Now the necessity in question here is not objective, 'such as would let us cognise *a priori* that everyone *will* feel this delight in the object that is called beautiful by me',[44] yet neither is it 'practical', that is, a pleasure that necessarily arises through the will's determination by the moral law. Rather it is exemplary—'a necessity of the assent of *all* to a judgement regarded as exemplifying a universal rule incapable of formulation'.[45]

On these terms, the necessity of a judgement of taste is conditional, and consists in the fact that, in asserting, say, 'This *x* is beautiful', we are thereby demanding that all others ought to find it so. While our demand is putatively justified because of its grounding in a 'universal rule' (or, as Kant puts it in §21, a 'common sense'), we must, nevertheless, ask what this rule or 'common sense' consists in. This brings us, in effect, to the point at which Kant left his Deduction in the Second Moment. But

[44] Ibid. 51.   [45] Ibid. 51.

Kant now goes on, in § 21, to provide the arguments which are the very core of the Deduction. These can be summarized in terms of the following points (i) Cognitions, judgements, and their attendant psychological states of conviction or belief must be universally communicable, otherwise true judgements (i.e. a correspondence of cognition with its object[46]) would not be possible. (ii) That which is universally communicable in cognition includes the subject's 'mental state'. This state involves two features; (a) the faculties of cognition (i.e. understanding and imagination) being in general accord with one another; (b) these faculties being combined in a proportion relative to the nature of the object cognized. (iii) There must be one such universally communicable proportion which is most conducive to stimulating the general accord of the faculties. (iv) This stimulated accord can only be recognized through the feeling of pleasure it gives rise to. (v) Since this pleasure arises from a 'common sense' (i.e. a mental state which is universally communicable), it too is universally communicable, and we are, therefore, justified in our demand that others ought to assent to the judgement of taste which we pronounce upon it.

Let me now consider this argument in greater depth. First, whatever the brevity of its exposition, point (i) is at least plausible, in that the possibility of making true judgements presupposes both a common capacity to apply concepts, and a common capacity for conviction or belief—whereby successful applications are recognized. However, the 'mental state' which Kant considers in point (ii) leads him into altogether murkier waters. For example, sub-points (ii*a*) and (ii*b*) are initially given a basically logical articulation. For cognition to be universally communicable, we 'must' suppose that both the faculties' disposition to be in accord and their specific proportion in an occurrent state of cognition (whereby this disposition is manifest) are, themselves, universally communicable—otherwise 'knowledge, as an effect [i.e. the recognition of true judgement] would not arise'.[47] Kant then repeats this argument in the guise of a description of what, psychologically speaking, 'actually happens' in cognition:

---

[46] Cf. the discussion of error in Kant, *Pure Reason*, B83/A59, pp. 97–8.
[47] Kant, *Judgement*, 83.

a given object, through the intervention of sense, sets the imagination at work in arranging the manifold, and the imagination, in turn, the understanding in giving to this arrangement the unity of concepts. But this disposition of the cognitive powers has a relative proportion differing with the diversity of the Objects that are given.[48]

Having thus transposed point (ii) into psychological terms, Kant continues in this vein, and is able to make the two crucial moves (points (iii) and (v)) which are the very heart of his transcendental deduction.

However, there must be one [i.e. proportionate relation of the faculties] in which this internal ratio suitable for quickening (one faculty by the other) is best adapted for both mental powers in respect of cognition (of given objects) generally, and this disposition can only be determined through feeling.[49]

It is important to bear in mind here that all that Kant has putatively established in point (ii) is that the disposition of the faculties to be in accord, and their specific proportion in an occurrent cognition, are universally communicable in the sense of being logical conditions of the possibility of true judgement. But in points (iii) and (v) Kant makes two crucial claims which in conjunction take him beyond what has been established by his transcendental argument. These claims are: first, that only one proportion in the relation of the faculties is best suited to stimulating the feeling of their harmonious accord, and, second, that the feeling caused by this proportion is universally communicable. In relation to the first of these, it is worth recalling that, for Kant, the proportion of the faculties is relative to 'the diversity of the objects that are given'. By this I take Kant to mean that the proportion of the faculties varies according to the contrasting phenomenal configurations that characterize different sorts of object. Hence, if (though Kant asserts rather than argues this point) only one proportion of the faculties is best suited to promoting their harmony, it follows that only one sort of phenomenal configuration can be beautiful. The question is, which? Kant does not clarify this issue in § 21 (or for that matter anywhere else in Book I of the third *Critique*), but there is a remark at the beginning of the Critique of Teleological Judgement which casts light on what he must have had in mind

---

[48] Ibid. 83.   [49] Ibid. 83–4.

here. We are told that there are 'Forms' 'which by their combination of unity and heterogeneity serve as it were to strengthen and entertain the mental powers . . . and to them the name of *beautiful forms* is given'.[50] However, while on these terms phenomenal configurations which combine unity with diversity are the embodiments of that proportion which best promotes the harmony of the faculties, one must ask how such a proportion is experienced in practice. In this respect, it has to be noted that, if one's capacities for cognitive discrimination have been cultivated and educated, one may be more sensitive and discerning in one's discrimination of what counts as unity and diversity than a person whose capacities have not been so developed. This means that, even if we must assume a common likeness of the faculties on transcendental grounds, and even if a particular judgement of taste is disinterested and focused on formal qualities of unity and diversity alone, there still remains scope for considerable divergence of response according to difference in cultivation amongst the individuals concerned. Our feeling of pleasure in the beautiful, therefore, cannot claim universal communicability. To establish this, Kant would have to supplement his position with arguments (à la Hume) to show the existence of a *standard of taste*; but this would take him beyond strictly a priori considerations.

The difficulties I have raised here are not at all obviated in § 38, where Kant offers his very brief official 'Deduction of judgements of taste'. We are told that if a pleasure arises from cognition of the formal aspects of an object alone, then the ground of this pleasure can only be due to 'the subjective conditions of judgement in general'.[51] This is that 'mental state' or 'common sense' which receives its fullest exposition in § 21. Indeed, the only new point of any substance in the official Deduction is contained in a footnote. Specifically, it holds that the subjective conditions of cognition 'are identical with all men' (i.e. universally communicable), otherwise communication would not be possible. Unfortunately, all that this new transcendental argument achieves is the reinforcement of points (i) and (ii) noted in relation to § 21. It does nothing to establish that the existence of a single, universally communicable, proportion of

---

[50] Kant, *Judgement*, Part II, p. 3.   [51] Ibid. Part I, p. 146.

the faculites is a sufficient condition for our pleasure in the beautiful having valid claim to universal communicability. Kant's basic failing here is, I would suggest, due to his making the unwarranted inference that, because the faculties capacity to be in accord and to combine in specific proportions is a *logical* condition of any cognition, then it must also determine the particular *psychological* process whereby the individual discriminates and responds with a feeling of pleasure to that proportion which is relevant to judgements of taste. Kant falls prey, in other words, to the ambiguous relation between the logical and psychological which is inherent in his very notion of the transcendental.

It will have been noticed that in this section my approach to Kant's arguments has been rather more critical than hitherto. The reason for this is due to questions raised about the Deduction by R. K. Elliot.[52] Having criticized Kant on grounds roughly similar to my own, he suggests that Kant's position is so weak that he must have been aware of the inadequacy of his arguments in § 21. Given also that, in § 22, Kant goes on to suggest that the question of whether the common sense is constitutive or regulative has not yet been decided, Elliot claims that the real foundation on which Kant must ultimately justify taste's claim to universal validity is its dependence on morality. In general terms Elliot's claim is true. However, his description of how the connection is made is not only extremely unwieldy and fundamentally implausible[53] but also presents Kant's position as rather more complete and assured than is, in fact, the case. In particular, Elliot misconstrues the crucial role played by § 59 ('Beauty as a symbol of morality') and the final paragraph of § 60. To rectify this situation, I shall begin by arguing that all the materials requisite for the completion of the Deduction are present in § 22 and § 40.

First, despite his presenting § 21 as a self-contained structure of argument, it is true that Kant was not himself entirely convinced that it constituted a sufficient basis for the Deduction.

[52] R. K. Elliot, 'The Unity of Kant's "Critique of Aesthetic Judgement"', *British Journal of Aesthetics*, 8: 3 (1968), 244–59.

[53] My most important reason for claiming this is that, while Kant again and again stresses the importance of the arguments in § 21, in Elliot's reading this section appears superfluous.

This becomes clear in the rather difficult § 22. Kant presents his central claims here in one continuous passage, but to be understood they must first be considered as individual units of argument—which I will signify through the use of numbered square brackets. First, having claimed that the common sense is a 'mere ideal norm', Kant goes on to ask (i) ['does . . . a common sense exist as a constitutive principle of the possibility of experience, or is it formed for us as a regulative principle] (ii) [by a still higher principle of reason that for higher ends first seeks to beget in us a common sense?] (iii) [Is taste, in other words, a natural and original faculty, or is it only the idea of one that is artificial and to be acquired by us, so that a judgement of taste, with its demand for universal assent, is but a requirement of reason for generating such a *consensus* . . .?'].[54]

Point (i) is the most important move here, but Kant rather misleadingly presents the common sense's possible constitutive *or* regulative status as if the two are mutually exclusive. They are not. § 21 with its description of what 'actually happens' shows that the existence of a common sense (construed as a harmonious and proportionate combination of the faculties) is in fact subjectively necessary and therefore constitutive of the possibility of experience. This, indeed, is all that § 21 establishes. However, in relation to its role in the judgement of taste (which, we will recall, involves only our consciousness of a feeling of pleasure) the common sense has a more ambiguous status. The reason for this is that, while the existence of a common sense is constitutive for experience as such, the fact that any particular instance of aesthetic pleasure actually has its causal origin in such a common sense is (despite Kant's mode of presentation in § 21) something which cannot be conclusively demonstrated. *If* we want our judgement of taste to have universal validity, *then* we must at least assume that it is causally grounded in the common sense, in the way described in § 21. But the question then arises as to why taste's claim to universal validity has anything *more* than this conditional status. One possibility open to Kant would be to say that, since the assumption of taste's origin in a common sense is coherent and serves to systematize our knowledge, it can be regarded as an a priori principle of theoretical reason. Yet since

[54] *Judgement*, 85.

the existence of that which such principles assume cannot be conclusively demonstrated, Kant may have thought that this would simply set the problem back one remove. A better approach would be to claim that the common sense is in effect a regulative principle of practical reason, since while, again, the existence of the things which such principles assume cannot be proven, their link with the presuppositions of morality gives us nevertheless positive reason to assert their existence. It is something on these lines, I would suggest, which Kant has in mind in § 22. Crucial in this respect is the meaning of point (ii). Kant suggests here that our very possession of a common sense is due ultimately to its connection with 'higher ends' of reason. To see what this means we must look ahead to a second definition of the common sense offered in § 40. Here we are told that it is

a *public* sense, i.e. a critical faculty which in its reflective act takes account (*a priori*) of the mode of representation of everyone else, in order, *as it were*, to weigh its judgement with the collective reason of mankind, and thereby avoid the illusion arising from subjective and personal conditions which could readily be taken for objective, an illusion that would exert a prejudicial influence upon its judgement.[55]

On these terms the common sense is not just a subjectively necessary condition of any experience. Rather, it is also able to function as a regulative principle in so far as the assumption of it—in those contexts where we aspire towards consensus but are inhibited by our sensuous particularity—serves *actively to dispose* our judgements towards universality. In assuming such a common sense in relation to judgement of taste, therefore, we not only have a coherent causal explanation of the grounds and universal validity of such judgements, but also, more conclusively, an assumption which, in itself, leads us to cultivate our rational, universalizing aspect. With these considerations in mind, we can now place point (iii) from § 22 in a proper perspective. Kant asks whether taste is a 'natural faculty' or something which is acquired through cultivation, in order (by means of our assumption of the common sense as a regulative principle) to generate consensus. Again, the two possibilities presented here are not mutually exclusive. On the one hand the causal account of taste's origin in the common sense (offered in

[55] Ibid. 151.

§ 21) shows how it *can* be theoretically explained as a natural faculty; and, on the other hand, the claims in § 40 about how the very assumption of this sort of origin promotes our rational, consensus-seeking being show why it *ought* to be cultivated. (The full significance of this latter point will become clear in a few moments.)

This brings us to the point at which Kant could have explicitly completed the Deduction. The essential move here would be to claim that, since the assumption of the common sense as a regulative principle promotes our capacity for elevating judgements beyond the sensuous and towards the universal, and since such a capacity is itself presupposed by morality, then (on a broad analogy with the other Ideas of Pure Practical Reason) this gives us positive grounds for believing that taste must in fact have its causal origin in a common sense, in the way described in § 21. This means, therefore, that the Deduction has two fundamental components—the causal account offered in § 21 and the morally conducive effects of assuming this account to be true. These *in conjunction* justify the judgement of taste's claim to universal validity. However, if—as seems the case—Kant is tending towards an answer of this sort, why is it that his approach is so tentative and halting, and why does he fail to make the final step absolutely explicit? Kant's reticence here, can, I think, be explained as follows. Early on in the third *Critique*, he is at pains to stress that the logical grounds of taste are entirely independent of those of the 'good'.[56] But in the context of the Introduction (and in relation to the notion of the 'final end' in particular) it is clear that the reason why there is such a thing as taste in the first place is to bridge the gulf between nature and freedom in a way that allows the former indirectly to promote the ends of the latter. From the *logical* viewpoint, taste is independent of morality, but in the *metaphysical* scheme of things, it exists to serve morality. If Kant had given an exhaustive and complete account of the Deduction on the lines suggested above, taste's metaphysical connection with morality might have seemed so pervasive as to impinge on its logically distinctive grounds. The reason for this is not only that it is a link with morality which finally clinches the justification of taste's claim to universal validity, but also, indeed,

[56] See e.g. § 4 (ibid.).

the fact that what this link compels us to assume as true (namely taste's causal origin in the common sense) is *itself* of moral significance. Kant begins to point us in this direction in his *Solution to the Antinomy of Taste* in § 57. Here he is fundamentally concerned with the ground of that which forms the causal component of taste's claim to universal validity, that is, with the question of what determines the common sense (through bringing the faculties into a harmonious and definite proportion). His answer is the a priori principle of reflective judgement. This (Kant now makes explicit) is a manifestation of our *supersensible* being. In the Critical philosophy generally, theoretical and moral principles are both manifestations of the 'supersensible'; but in the third *Critique* he uses the term in a more fundamental sense to pick out that unity[57] which links these two domains together so as to realize morality's status as the final end of all creation. Hence, in so far as it is the a priori principle of reflective judgement which manifests this morally significant unifying aspect of the supersensible, and in so far as taste has its causal origin in a common sense which is determined by this principle, it follows that taste's causal origin is itself of ultimately moral significance. These considerations would clearly place Kant in a difficult position. To make morality's link with both components of the Deduction too explicit too soon might seem to weaken his claims to having established taste on logically distinctive grounds. This, I would suggest, is why Kant does not really address the significance of morality for the Deduction until § 59 and § 60 (the two very final sections of the Critique of Aesthetic Judgement). Even here, however (as I shall now show), he stresses taste's relation to only one of the two morally significant factors, and even then in a somewhat misleading way.

Kant begins § 59 by considering the semantic relations between intuitions and concepts. There are two varieties. First, a *signifying* relation holds when mere 'marks' denote concepts

---

[57] Elliot (op. cit. (n. 52 above), 257) suggests that the unity in question is God. This is probably correct. It is he who we presume to have created the phenomenal world and our rational moral being so as to allow the ends of the latter to be realized. That which bridges these two realms in accordance with the Divinely ordained final end is the a priori principle of regulative judgement. This is why, I would suggest, in the Critique of Teleological Judgement Kant describes the aesthetic pleasure which arises from such a principle as 'akin to a *religious* feeling' (*Judgement*, Part II, p. 159).

without their having anything structurally in common with the objects intuited under that concept. In a *symbolic* relation matters are somewhat more complex:

judgement performs a double function: first in applying the concept to an object of sensible intuition, and then, secondly, in applying the mere rule of its reflection to quite another object, of which the former is but the symbol.[58]

For example, a monarchical state is symbolized by a body when it is constitutional, and by a handmill when it is absolute. Kant supposes that, in such cases, there is something structurally in common between the way judgement unifies the parts in a manifold of intuition (i.e. as a body, or as a handmill) and the way, in thought, judgement unifies the parts of an idea (i.e. as a constitutional, or absolute, monarchy).

The many obscurities of this theory need not detain us. It is sufficient to note that, for Kant, symbolic relations hold by virtue of analogical structure between judgements. This brings us to the most crucial passages of § 59. Rather than expound these in depth, I will first briefly survey the ostensible structure of Kant's argument. Again it can be reduced to five points. (i) Only in so far as it is a symbol of the morally good can beauty give rise to a pleasure that claims universal assent. (ii) This pleasure makes us aware of the superiority of our rational side over our merely sensuous being. (iii) It can do this because it is universally valid, through being founded (like morality) on an a priori and, thereby, supersensible determining ground. (iv) Pure aesthetic judgements are analogous with moral judgements, in respect of their characteristics of immediacy, disinterestedness, and universality. (v) The analogy between beauty and morality is borne out by common usage.

The establishing of point (i), here, is generally held to be the whole *raison d'être* of § 59; but it raises some particularly acute problems of interpretation. Donald Crawford suggests that Kant's basic intention is to show that

. . . our judgements marking the pleasure in the beautiful . . . can rightly demand universal assent, not simply because they can be based on what

---

[58] Elliot (op cit. (n. 52 above), 257), Part I, p. 222.

can be universally communicated, but because they mark an experience of that which symbolises morality.[59]

If this were Kant's point, then § 59 would not so much *complete* the Deduction (as Crawford holds) but would constitute a logically independent *supplement* to it. However, there is good reason to believe that this is not Kant's basic intention, anyway. For example, the passage in which (i) is asserted reads as follows:

the beautiful is the symbol of the morally good, and *only in this light* [my emphasis] (a point of view natural to every one, and which every one exacts from others as a duty) does it give us pleasure with an attendant claim to the agreement of everyone.[60]

A literal interpretation of the very strong wording in this passage would suggest that an awareness of beauty's symbolizing of morality is not (*contra* Crawford) simply an additional ground which would justify the claim to universality, but is rather a causal condition of our pleasure in the beautiful having any claim to universal validity at all. Unfortunately, this literal interpretation itself comes up against two major problems. First, it would suggest that the structure of argument which Kant offers in § 59 is radically incomplete, for while points (iii) and (iv) show how beauty can and does symbolize morality, they do not (even in conjunction with points (ii) and (v)) show that it *must* do so, in order to give rise to a universally valid pleasure. Second, if the literal interpretation were correct, then it would entail (at the very least) a very drastic revision of the Deduction in order to accommodate the causal role of our awareness of beauty's necessary connection with morality. There is, however, an alternative approach to the literal interpretation of point (i). The clue for this is provided by the problem of how taste's claim to universality fares in the absence of a knowledge of Kant's Critical philosophy (i.e. amongst the vast majority of those who exercise taste). One presumes that, in the absence of a knowledge of the ground covered by the Deduction, the claim to universality is either blind or made on the wrong grounds. We need, therefore, something of more general significance which the third *Critique* has not yet provided—namely an accessible route

[59] Donald Crawford, *Kant's Aesthetic Theory* (University of Wisconsin Press: Madison, 1974), 156.
[60] *Judgement*, Part I, pp. 223–4.

towards awareness of the grounds on which the judgement of taste's claim to universal validity can be based. With this in mind, I would suggest that Kant's literal position in point (i) is simply a misleading statement of a less ambitious thesis—that (in the absence of a knowledge of the third *Critique*) it is only in so far as beauty symbolizes morality that it is able to give rise to a pleasure which can be recognized as having grounds for claiming the agreement of everyone. To put this more precisely, the role of the symbolic relation to morality is to make us conscious of that supersensible ground which sustains the common sense and provides the causal component in the judgement of taste's claim to universal validity. This interpretation of point (i) not only fills a gap in Kant's general position and avoids the difficulties of the literal interpretation, but also gives continuity to the remaining structure of argument in § 59 in a way that shows it to be crucial to the overall strategy of the third *Critique*. To see why this is so, let us commence from point (ii)—Kant's claim that our universally valid pleasure in the beautiful enables the mind to become 'conscious of a certain enoblement and elevation above mere sensibility to pleasure from impressions of sense'.

Whether this awareness *always* arises from our pleasure in the beautiful is left ambiguous. However, the very fact that it *can* do so is one whose possibility Kant goes on immediately to explain, through point (iii). First, we are told that, in this awareness of ennoblement, taste 'extends its view' to the 'intelligible'. By 'intelligible' here Kant means that unifying supersensible *ground* which (by means of the a priori principle of reflective judgement) links the domain of natural concepts with that of freedom, in a way that enables the former indirectly to promote the ends of the latter. Kant then further articulates the relation between this notion and taste by means of the following passage. The 'intelligible', we are told, is that which

brings even our higher cognitive faculties into common accord, and is that apart from which sheer contradiction would arise between their nature and the claims put forward by taste. In this faculty judgement does not find itself subjected to a heteronomy of laws of experience as it does in the empirical estimate of things . . . it gives the law to itself.[61]

---

[61] *Judgement*, Part I, pp. 224.

On these terms, the 'intelligible' is at the root of that a priori principle of reflective judgement which combines the faculties in a harmonious and definite proportion in a way that gives rise to the judgement of taste. It is, indeed, only the (morally conducive) assumption of this causal origin which justifies the judgement of taste's claim to universal validity. Given this supersensible determining ground in an a priori principle, the judgement of taste is not restricted by any empirical concept of the object's end. It is, rather (to use Kant's term from earlier on in the third *Critique*), 'heautonomous', that is akin to theoretical and pure practical reason in its supersensible foundation, but unlike them in so far as it is not constitutive for any phenomenal or rational object. As Kant puts it, taste 'finds a reference to something in the Subject itself and outside it, and which is not nature, nor yet freedom, but is still connected with the ground of the latter, i.e. the supersensible'.[62]

Now the step which Kant is taking here, in point (iii), is, in effect, a repetition of the major claim in his solution to the Antinomy of Taste—namely that the universal validity of the judgement of taste is only possible through our assuming it to have a priori supersensible grounding. By repeating this conclusion here, Kant is able to establish the possibility of point (ii), that is, show why beauty *can* make us conscious of being elevated above the merely sensuous. But what he has not yet done is to clarify the actual process whereby we do become thus conscious. We will remember that, for Kant, the harmony of the faculties achieved through the judgement of taste can only be recognized through a feeling of pleasure. If our 'common conviction' of the universal validity of judgements of taste is to be justified, and if we are to feel elevated above mere pleasures of sense, then we must not only *feel* aesthetic pleasure, but must also have some awareness of its origin. This means that our judgement of taste must in some way actually refer to its assumed supersensible ground; but how is this semantic relation possible? Now from a modern viewpoint there is no real difficulty here, inasmuch as we could say that the judgement of taste 'exemplifies' (in something like Nelson Goodman's sense of 'possession plus reference')[63] its supersensible ground. For example, just as

[62] Ibid. 224.
[63] See Nelson Goodman, *Languages of Art* (Hackett & Co: Indianapolis, 1976), 53.

(through its possession of specific stylistic qualities) a vase exemplifies its origin as a product of the Meissen factory, so too does the judgement of taste (through its logical characteristics of immediacy and disinterestedness, etc.) exemplify a supersensible causal origin. However, this very direct semantic route is not open to Kant, for two reasons. First, the relevant feature of his semantic theory—namely symbolic relations—does not encompass exemplification, but holds only by virtue of analogies between judgements. Second, early on in the third *Critique* Kant suggests that the supersensible is only 'cognisable' through 'freedoms formal laws' (i.e. morality).[64] One presumes that the reason for this is that, even if we are aware of Kant's Critical philosophy, theoretical reason can only posit the supersensible in negative terms. The presupposition of morality, in contrast, leads us to affirm the supersensible in a more positive way—as the domain of freedom, God, and immortality. Indeed, even if one is not familiar with Kant's philosophy, it is nevertheless true that in practice morality often involves us acting against our sensuous inclinations, and is commonly supposed to determine both one's fate in an afterlife and one's relationship to God. It is morality which is the most accessible route to our supersensible aspect. Linking these two points together, it is clear that if we are to become conscious of the supersensible ground whose assumption validates the universality of the judgement of taste, and which also serves to ennoble us above mere sensuous pleasure, this could only be achieved through a symbolic relation between the characteristics of, and claims we make for, judgements of taste, and those embodied in judgements of morality. This is why, having repeated the supersensible basis of taste and the claims made for it in point (iii), Kant goes on, in points (iv) and (v), to show that judgements of taste and morality are, in fact, analogous in four key respects, and that common usage gives a broader sustenance to this analogy.

I am arguing, then, that the structure of argument which Kant presents in § 59 can only be made sense of if we take Kant to be establishing that only in so far as beauty is a symbol of the morally good can we become conscious of the supersensible ground whose assumption (with its morally conducive effects)

[64] Kant, *Judgement*, 11.

justifies the ascription of universal validity to the judgement of taste. On these terms, the real significance of § 59 is to provide a clarification of the only way in which (independently of a knowledge of Kant's philosophy) we can become conscious of what the Deduction 'proves'. All the major difficulties of this section stem, therefore, from Kant's talking as though an awareness of beauty's symbolizing of morality were a causal condition of our aesthetic pleasure itself, rather than of our understanding of its origin. That he should make this mistake is, I would suggest, due to the fact that what the symbolic relation makes us aware of is a causal ground that (as I showed earlier) is *itself* of moral significance.

Let me now, in conclusion, clarify the full significance of § 59. First, while we have a common conviction of taste's universality, this is not a sufficient condition for validating that claim. We need also to back it up with some coherent idea about how taste has the appropriate sort of causal ground. While this is provided by Kant through his notion of the common sense in § 21, in § 59 he moves deeper still by showing how we can become aware of that which, in turn, grounds the common sense—namely the supersensible. The *effect* of this awareness, however, is the same as that of our assumption of the common sense, inasmuch as it shows that we can assume taste's causal ground to be other than that of our sensuous particularity. Hence, just as at the technical level of the Deduction the assumption of a common sense disposes us to aspire towards universality in our judgements, so too (one presumes) the assumption of taste's supersensible grounding will dispose us to the universal. The arguments concerning beauty as a symbol of morality show how an equivalent of the Deduction might operate outside the specialized context of a knowledge of the Critical philosophy. The significance of this is not just to show how the common man can with confidence claim universality for his judgements of taste; it also enables Kant, *at last*, to show something of the metaphysical depth that characterizes taste's connection with morality. On the one hand, we can suppose that an awareness of taste's grounding in the supersensible will dispose us to cultivate our morally significant capacity for universalizing; and on the other hand, the very fact that we *are* made aware of our supersensible aspect is, in itself, the presentation of a morally significant idea. Given this, it

is hardly surprising that in the very final paragraph of the
Critique of Aesthetic Judgement Kant should say that

> taste is, in the ultimate analysis, a critical faculty that judges of the
> rendering of moral ideas in terms of sense (through the intervention of a
> certain analogy in our reflection on both); and it is this rendering also,
> and the increased sensibility, founded upon it, for the feeling which
> these ideas evoke . . . that are the origin of that pleasure which taste
> declares valid for mankind in general.[65]

I would elaborate this passage as follows. First, beauty's
symbolic relation to morality is here assigned its proper *mediating*
role. It enables taste as a critical (i.e. consensus engendering)
faculty to render moral ideas (presumably pertaining to the
supersensible). The very fact that beauty can thus promote a
morally significant capacity and present moral ideas is (as we
have seen) the reason why its claim to universal validity is
justified. However, this twofold function is also metaphysically
speaking the 'origin' and *raison d'être* of taste itself. The fact that
such morally significant notions arise in the context of 'sense' as
well as in specifically moral contexts makes us all the more
susceptible to moral feeling. Hence we find that an aspect of our
natural being, determined by the principle of natural finality, is
ultimately of indirect service to morality. Thus Kant realizes the
fundamental strategy of the third *Critique*—to bridge the gulf
between nature and freedom in a way that shows the former
indirectly to promote the ends of the latter. Taste exists, in other
words, to serve the final end.

Kant's arguments concerning the epistemological and moral
significance of taste have little to recommend them in any
systematic way. To accept them we would have to undertake
the daunting task of revising some of the most problematic
concepts in the whole of the Critical philosophy—such as the
supersensible and the final end. Indeed, even within the terms of
his own philosophy, Kant's Deduction is not successful in
meeting the difficulties I noted earlier. For even if the assumption
of taste's causal origin in the common sense is morally conducive
and the source of moral ideas, this only has the effect of giving all
judgements of taste which strive towards universality (and which
satisfy the other formal conditions) equal claim to universal

[65] Kant, *Judgement*, 227.

validity. But, as I showed in the critical discussion of § 21, it is possible for a judgement of taste to have such features and yet still elicit contradictory responses on the basis of the different levels to which individuals have cultivated their taste. Of course, a particularly cultivated person might claim the assent of others to his judgement as a duty, in so far as, by educating their taste to his standard, they improve their own talents and thereby fulfil a duty to themselves. Yet this claim would not be justified unless the person in question could prove his possession of such high powers of discrimination by discussing and comparising examples of beautiful form. This, however, would take us beyond a priori considerations. Despite these drawbacks, Kant's arguments remain sources of scattered insights, and I will consider some particularly worthwhile points in later chapters.

Having provided an exposition of Kant's aesthetic theory and its relation to the overall moral dimension of the third *Critique*, I am now in a position to clarify how, in that work, the notion of the sublime deriving from the Critical ethics is translated back into aesthetic terms. This will be the very heart of my study.

4

Kant's Analytic of the Sublime: From the Preliminary Sections to the Mathematical Mode

I

The second book of Part I of the *Critique of Judgement* is called the 'Analytic of the Sublime' and extends from § 23 to § 54, inclusively. That Kant should give this title to the second book is extremely puzzling, inasmuch as only §§ 23 to 30 are concerned explicitly with the question of sublimity. Kant's strategy here is at best complex and at worst obscure, and is due to the problematic relation in his theory between sublimity and art. (This relation is, indeed, so problematic that I shall defer discussion of it until after I have offered a reconstructed version of Kant's theory in Part III of this study.) In relation to those sections which are more directly addressed to the sublime, it should be noted that my treatment of these will for the moment be expository and interpretative, and will consider critical issues only in so far as they pertain to points not central to Kant's main argument; or in so far as they are directly raised *in* problems of interpretation. Let me now address, then, the opening sections of the Analytic of the Sublime.

Kant opens his discussion in § 23 with a comparison and contrast of judgements of the beautiful and the sublime. (As his arguments concentrate primarily on the points of contrast—and are somewhat contentious—I shall accordingly focus my attention on these.) Kant begins with the twofold claim that the beautiful and the sublime both please on their own account (i.e. in themselves rather than as means towards some other end), and both involve reflective judgements rather than judgements of sense or determinative judgements. From this, Kant supposes it to follow[1] that the delight which we take in them

---

[1] Or so at least Kant says. Strictly speaking, however, the inference is not valid in so far as the fact that the judgement involved is reflective rather than determinative

does not originate in sensation or a *definite* concept, but is, rather,

connected with the mere presentation or faculty of presentation [i.e. imagination], and is thus taken to express the accord in a given intuition, of the faculty of presentation, or the imagination, with the *faculty of concepts* that belongs to understanding or reason, in the sense of the former [i.e. imagination] assisting the latter.[2]

This allows us, in turn, to make a further inference, namely that judgements of the sublime and the beautiful are both singular, and both profess to claim universal validity. Kant then goes on to make his points of contrast. First,

The beautiful in nature is a question of the form of the object, and this consists in limitation, whereas the sublime is to be found in an object even devoid of form, so far as it immediately involves, or else by its presence provokes, a representation of limitlessness, yet with a super-added thought of its totality.[3]

The wording in the first part of this passage seems to suggest that the sublime can be experienced in relation to both objects with form and those which are formless. In practice, however, Kant concentrates on the latter sort. (Indeed in § 23 and elsewhere in the Analytic of the Sublime he even goes so far as to disallow art objects as a source of pure judgements of sublimity, in so far as their form can only be grasped in relation to definite concepts of an end.) What Kant has in mind by the term 'formless' can be illustrated as follows. If we view a mountain in the distance it has a characteristic shape which enables us to decribe it as 'a mountain'. But suppose that we are standing at its base with, perhaps, its higher reaches shrouded in mist. Under these conditions we lack the vantage-point which would dispose us simply to describe it as 'a mountain'. Rather, our perceptual faculties cannot take in the sheer immensity of the peak. They are swamped. The mountain seems, in our close and immediate perceptual encounter with it, to be a limitless phenomenal mass or aggregate, without any overall defining shape or form. Again,

does not *of itself* rule out a definite concept being involved. To establish this, Kant should have placed his comments about the accord of the faculty of concepts immediately before his remarks about the beautiful and sublime not presupposing any definite concept.

[2] *Judgement*, Book II, § 23, p. 90.   [3] Ibid. 90.

suppose that the peak is one of a series. Here, while the individual 'mountains' may (from a distance) be characterizable as such without difficulty, it may be that our attention is engrossed by the perceptual rhythm of the series—its seeming to flow beyond the horizon towards infinity. In these two examples we see how an object can appear to be formless by overwhelming our perceptual faculties and suggesting the idea of limitlessness or infinity to us. The fact that formless objects are encountered in terms of such 'representations' is Kant's second point in the last quoted passage. Indeed this point of contrast between beauty's orientation towards form and sublimity's orientation towards formlessness is already hinted at in the preceding paragraph, where Kant links the former to a harmony of imagination and understanding, and the latter to a harmony of imagination and *reason*. For Kant generally (as we have seen) understanding is a faculty for forming rules or concepts, whereas reason seeks to systematize concepts by grounding them in more comprehensive general principles. The drive to bring about such systematization is what we have previously encountered as the 'interest of theoretical reason'. It is interesting, however, that, in the third *Critique*, Kant *stresses* the extremely broad scope of this notion. It is not only operative in relation to the organization of bodies of empirical knowledge, but even makes demands at the direct level of sensible intuition. As Kant remarks in § 27, 'the idea of the comprehension of any phenomenon whatsoever, that may be given us, in a whole of intuition, is an idea imposed on us by a law of reason'.[4] It is reason's demand for such a presentation of totality which (as becomes clear in §§ 25 and 26) is operative in relation to formless objects. This demand launches the imagination into a vain attempt to comprehend the magnitude of the formless phenomenon in a way that leads ultimately to the suggestion of a 'super-added' idea of 'totality'. Kant accordingly concludes his first point of contrast by noting that, whereas our delight in the beautiful is 'coupled' with a representation of Quality, our pleasure in the sublime involves a representation of Quantity.

Given these contrasts, it is hardly surprising that Kant then goes on to claim that at the subjective level the *feeling* of the

---

[4] *Judgement*, Book II, § 27, p. 105.

beautiful and that of the sublime have different phenomenological structures. Our pleasure in the former involves 'a feeling of the furtherance of life'[5] which is compatible with charm, and the playfulness of imagination. Our pleasure in the sublime, in contrast,

is a pleasure that only arises indirectly, being brought about by a momentary check to the vital forces followed at once by a discharge all the more powerful, and so it is an emotion that seems to be no sport, but dead earnest in the affairs of imagination.[6]

This initial characterization of the feeling of the sublime seems relatively straightforward. Imagination's adequacy to cope with the formless phenomenon involves a sense of pain—a 'check to the vital forces'. This is succeeded by a powerful sense of relief (perhaps even elation) in so far as the formless phenomenon *can* be grasped as a totality in terms of a rational idea. Kant then complicates his position by going on to suggest that

since the mind is not simply attracted by the object, but is alternately repelled thereby, the delight in the sublime does not so much involve positive pleasure as admiration or respect, i.e. merits the name of a negative pleasure.[7]

The particular interest of this passage (in conjunction with the previously quoted one) is that it offers the first glimmering of an ambiguity that besets the rest of Kant's discussion of the sublime.[8] In the first passage, Kant talks as though the experience of the sublime involves two distinct stages—one negative, the other positive. In the second passage, however, he talks as though the experience is much more complex—involving *alternations* of attraction and repulsion towards the object. While I shall deal with the questions raised by this ambiguity in more detail in Section III of Chapter 5 in this study, it will be useful briefly to highlight the more fundamental issue from which it arises through considering Kant's next and most important point of contrast between the beautiful and the sublime.

The substance of Kant's point concerns the *grounding* of beauty's and sublimity's different phenomenological structures.

---

[5] Ibid. 91.　　　[6] Ibid. 91.　　　[7] Ibid. 91.

[8] Esp. in § 27 in relation to the feeling of the sublime, and in § 29 in his summary 'Deduction' of judgements of sublimity.

To understand his position we must first recall that our pleasure in the beautiful is caused by an object's form bringing about a harmony of the cognitive faculties on the basis of the reflective judgement's a priori principle of natural finality. In the case of judgements of sublimity, in contrast, the object seems

in point of form to contravene the ends of our power of judgement, to be ill adapted to our faculty of presentation, and to be, as it were, an outrage on the imagination, and yet it is judged all the more sublime on that account.[9]

Kant's point here is that, if an object is formless, our imagination has so much difficulty in grasping its manifold that the object seems to defeat the very end of cognition itself. It is, as Kant goes on to put it, 'contra-final'.[10] This leads him to claim that 'we express ourselves on the whole inaccurately if we term any *Object of nature* sublime, although we may with perfect propriety call many such objects beautiful'.[11]

Kant's reasoning here is based on the fact that, if the formless natural object is contra-final, we can only explain the pleasure we take in it in so far as 'the object lends itself to the presentation of a sublimity discoverable in the mind'.[12] Indeed, 'the sublime, in the strict sense of the word, cannot be contained in any sensuous form, but rather concerns ideas of reason'.[13]

On these terms, that which is sublime is not the formless object itself, but rather the *supersensible* cast of mind which, through ideas of reason, can grasp the totality suggested by such objects. The way Kant uses this point is, however, somewhat misleading. In the case of judgements of taste and sublimity objects of nature play in fact a broadly similar role. It is not they *as such* which are the ground of our pleasure, but rather the way in which they engage our cognitive faculties. It is in the details of this latter point that the real basis of Kant's contrast is to be found. Again, I shall comment on it at more length in section III of Chapter 5 of this study.

Let me now consider the final point of contrast which Kant draws with beauty in § 23. We are told that

Self-subsisting natural beauty reveals to us a technic of nature which shows it in the light of a system ordered in accordance with laws the

---

[9] *Judgement*, Book II, § 27, p. 91.   [10] i.e. in relation to cognition.
[11] *Judgement*, 91–2.   [12] Ibid. 92.   [13] Ibid. 92.

principle of which is not to be found within the range of our entire faculty of understanding. This principle is that of a finality relative to the employment of judgement in respect of phenomena which have thus to be assigned not to nature regarded as aimless mechanism, but also to nature regarded after the analogy of art.[14]

Here Kant is suggesting that the appreciation of natural beauty can enlarge our concept of nature by making us aware that our understanding of it is teleological as well as mechanistic. This in turn invites 'profound inquiries' as to how such teleological understanding is possible. But in contrast to this, in 'what we are wont to call sublime in nature there is . . . an absence of anything leading to particular objective principles and corresponding forms of nature'.[15]

Kant explains this contrast by pointing out that, whereas beauty evidences the finality of nature and has a ground 'external' to the judging subject, the sublime has a finality 'independent' of nature, whose ground is 'in' the judging subject. From my observations on the second point of contrast (noted earlier) it is clear that Kant is again overstating his contrast, at the expense of the sublime. Apart from querying the appropriateness of the distinction between beauty's supposed 'external' and sublimity's supposed 'independent' grounding, one might also note that, even if the sublime does not lead to 'profound inquiries' as to the possibility of natural order, it surely does reveal equally important links between nature and our rational and moral being. Indeed it is altogether ironic that (as I showed in Chapter 3) by the end of the Critique of Aesthetic Judgement Kant switches the emphasis of his exposition, and attempts especially in the section entitled 'Beauty as a symbol of morality' to relate beauty to this selfsame rational and moral being. The metaphysical ground of its existence consists in the fact that it provides a bridging of the gulf between nature and freedom, in accordance with the final end. This means, in effect, that beauty's ultimate significance is in its having, like the sublime, a 'higher finality' in relation to *reason*.

Having made his introductory comparison and contrast in § 23, Kant goes on, in § 24, to outline the formal organization of his

[14] Ibid. 92.
[15] Ibid. 92. Kant is inconsistent here in allowing that we can regard nature in itself as sublime.

discussion of the sublime. Given the fact that, like beauty, the sublime involves a reflective judgement, Kant initially suggests that, as in the Analytic of the Beautiful, the Analytic of the Sublime must show its judgements to be in their Quantity universally valid; in their Quality, independent of interest; in their Relation, subjectively final; and in their Modality necessary. Now Kant suggests that the only difference between this and the earlier approach is that the Analytic of the Sublime should (for reasons mentioned in § 23) commence from the Moment of Quantity. Unfortunately, there are some rather more radical divergences than this small difference would immediately suggest. Only the Moment of Modality is construed by Kant in roughly the same sense in both the Analytic of the Beautiful and the Analytic of the Sublime. The other moments are given an altogether different interpretation, as follows. First, in the Analytic of the Beautiful, Quantity is construed as universality (i.e. the epistemological status of the judgement of taste). In § 23 and § 24 of the Analytic of the Sublime, however, Quantity is construed in a literal sense, as pertaining to the fact that the sublime involves an indeterminate idea of totality. Indeed, after § 24 it is dropped altogether (for reasons I will consider in a moment). Kant's treatment of Quality likewise undergoes radical change. In the Analytic of the Beautiful it is characterized by the disinterestedness of pure aesthetic judgements, whereas in the Analytic of the Sublime it is given a number of different usages. First, in § 23 Kant suggests that because the appreciation of beauty pertains to the *form* of objects it is a 'representation of Quality' (whereas, as we have seen, the sublime involves a representation of Quantity). In § 24, Kant nominally returns to his original usage, but then, in § 27, which explicitly deals with Quality, he offers a curious analysis based on the phenomenology of both the sublime reflective judgement and the feeling it embodies. It is only in the General Remarks, following § 29, that we again find a more substantial employment in its original usage. Matters pertaining to the Moment of Relation are equally complex; for while in § 24 Kant asserts that judgements of the sublime involve the Relation of subjective finality, he then provides no section or Moment to correspond to this.

Some of Kant's ambiguity in relation to these terms stems from the fact that 'the analysis of the sublime obliges a division not required by that of the beautiful, namely one into the mathematically and dynamically sublime'.[16]

The reason which Kant gives for this is that whereas our appreciation of the beautiful involves restful contemplation, our appreciation of the sublime involves a 'mental movement' combined with the estimate of the object. Given the suggestion in § 23 that in our experience of the sublime the mind is alternately attracted and repelled, one can understand why the sublime involves a mental movement. But this of itself does not explain why, in giving rise to the sublime, a formless object can be 'referred' to the faculties either of cognition or of desire; that is, it does not explain why a division into two different varieties of sublimity is called for. The real reason for this distinction only becomes clear after Kant has extensively discussed both varieties in § 26 and § 28 respectively. However, we can get a preliminary inkling of this by briefly considering the provenance of the terms 'mathematical' and 'dynamical' in the first *Critique*. In an important footnote to the Axioms of Intuition, Kant states that

the synthesis of the homogeneous in everything . . . can be *mathematically* treated. This synthesis can . . . be divided into that of *aggregation* and that of *coalition*, the former applying to *extensive* and the latter to *intensive* qualities. The second mode of combination (nexus) is the synthesis of the manifold so far as its constituents *necessarily belong to one another*, as, for example, the accident to some substance, or the effect to the cause. It is therefore synthesis of that which, though heterogeneous, is yet represented as combined *a priori*. This combination, as not being arbitrary, and as concerning the connection of the existence of the manifold, I entitle dynamical.[17]

It is clear that the extensive and intensive qualities of a whole which are involved in mathematical synthesis are the basis of the magnitude of phenomena (i.e. the proportion of space and time they occupy relative to other phenomena). The dynamical synthesis on the other hand pertains to the physical powers and cohesion of phenomena. How, then, can this distinction be of relevance to the sublime? The answer is that, while, as Kant makes clear in § 23 and elsewhere, the formlessness of phenomena can overwhelm perception and thus give rise to a rational idea, a similar idea can also be occasioned in us when a

---

[16] *Judgement*, Book II, § 27, p. 94.   [17] *Pure Reason*, B202, pp. 197–8.

great phenomenon threatens through its physical powers to overwhelm and completely destroy us. This means that a distinction between the mathematical and dynamic sublime is called for not because the sublime involves a mental movement, but because there are two different ways in which this movement can be set in motion.

Given these two distinct varieties of the sublime one would expect that each would be analysable in terms of its own particular moments of Quantity, Quality, and so forth. Yet the organization of Kant's discussion after § 24 is as follows.

   (i) § 25 and § 26—The Mathematical Sublime.
  (ii) § 27—Quality.
 (iii) § 28—The Dynamical Sublime.
 (iv) § 29—Modality.

In this structure Kant clearly treats the Mathematical and Dynamical as though they correspond to Moments of Quantity and Quality respectively. The reason why he takes this approach is either to conceal the differences between the two, or (more probably) for considerations of economy. To give the two varieties separate treatment would have made an already badly organized and repetitive exposition even more so. Objectively speaking, however, it is unfortunate that Kant did not take this risk, since, as his discussion stands, important differences between the mathematical and dynamical sublime are rather obscured. What these differences are will become clear as my study progresses.

With this overview of Kant's approach to the sublime before us, we can now proceed to the first of his more detailed articulations of it, namely the theory of the mathematical sublime.

II

Kant's expository discussion of the mathematical sublime is spread out over § 25, § 26, and § 27 of the third *Critique*. His organization of the discussion is somewhat awkward, and to make sense of it I will sometimes be obliged (especially in the latter part of this section) to depart from the order in which he presents his points of argument.

Kant opens § 25 with the following remarks.

Sublime is the name given to what is *absolutely great*. But to be great and to be a magnitude are entirely different concepts . . . . In the same way to *assert without qualification* (*simpliciter*) that something is great, is quite a different thing from saying that it is *absolutely great* . . . . The latter is *what is beyond all comparison great*.[18]

In these remarks, as well as formally defining the sublime as that which is absolutely great, Kant also wishes to make a contrast on the one hand between greatness and magnitude as such, and, on the other hand, between greatness and that which is absolutely and beyond all comparison great (i.e. the sublime). The bulk of § 25 is devoted to a consideration of these two contrasts, in turn. It is important to note first that what Kant means by 'great' (or great 'without qualification') is our capacity to estimate things informally 'by the eye',[19] rather than by mathematical measurement. He gives this informal mode of estimation, however, a somewhat complex characterization. It does not involve a 'pure concept of understanding' nor 'an intuition of sense' nor 'a concept of reason'; but is, rather, guided by a concept of judgement which involves 'subjective finality'. To show why this is so, Kant now proceeds to a major contrast—namely, between recognizing a magnitude as such and judging its greatness.

Given a multiplicity of the homogeneous together constituting one thing, and we may at once cognise from the thing itself that it is a magnitude (quantum). No comparison with other things is required.[20]

Kant's reasoning here stands in some need of explanation. In the first *Critique* he takes himself to have shown that to recognize something as a specific whole of intuition presupposes the successive apprehension of the homogeneous parts of its manifold. As he puts it, 'the representation of the parts makes possible, and therefore necessarily precedes the representation of the whole'.[21] It is this connective activity which, according to Kant, 'generates' a determinate spatio-temporal magnitude for the whole. Given, therefore, that the specific magnitude of particular items is generated in the very act of cognition, it is easy

---

[18] *Judgement*, § 25, p. 94.
[20] Ibid. § 25, p. 95.

[19] Ibid. § 26, p. 98.
[21] *Pure Reason*, B203, p. 198.

to understand why, in the third *Critique*, Kant suggests that we can recognize it without making comparisons with other magnitudes. What is rather more puzzling is the fact that, in § 25, Kant claims that this recognition is achieved 'at once'. One would have thought that if (in accordance with the first *Critique*'s position) we must successively apprehend all the parts in a manifold, then this (rather implausibly) will make the mere recognition of magnitude into a temporarily very prolonged process. Fortunately, in § 27 Kant shows that he has now revised his first *Critique* position in a way that avoids such an implausible consequence. We are told that, in relation to the act of apprehension, imagination can, by a 'subjective movement' of mind, do 'violence' to the inner-sense. Such a movement 'removes the time-condition in the progression of the imagination, and renders *co-existence* intuitable'.[22]

This means that we can recognize an object as having determinate magnitude immediately. However (returning now to § 25), to estimate *just how great* a particular magnitude is presupposes another condition—namely being measured against something else which itself has magnitude. This leads Kant to one of his most crucial points.

... since in the estimate of magnitude we have to take into account not merely the multiplicity (number of units) but also the magnitude of the unit (the measure), and since the magnitude of this unit in turn always requires something else as its measure, and as the computation of the magnitude of phenomena is, in all cases, utterly incapable of affording us any absolute conception of magnitude.[23]

Kant holds, then, that (i) the estimation of magnitude is always based on comparison; and (ii) that it can never be determined absolutely. These two points form, in effect, the main pivots for the progression of Kant's argument in § 25. He concentrates initially on (i). In the case of estimating something as great by 'the eye alone', 'greatness is ascribed to it pre-eminently among many other objects of a like kind, yet without the extent of this pre-eminence being [precisely] determined'.[24] Here the measure or standard used in the estimation of an object's magnitude is not linked to it by means of a definite, objective mathematical rule. It is, rather, derived informally,

---

[22] *Judgement*, § 27, p. 107.   [23] Ibid. § 25, p. 95.   [24] Ibid. 95.

either from empirical observation (e.g. our rough idea of the average size for a man or house), or 'given *a priori*'[25]—as in those cases (such as judging the greatness of a virtue) where the standard involved is a rational idea (i.e. a concept which cannot be adequately presented in intuition). Perhaps the most puzzling aspect of the account so far is why such estimates as these should be interpreted as cases of 'subjective finality'. In this respect, we will remember that for Kant judgements of finality involve relating some object to the 'concept of an end'—which is construed as the ground of the object's possibility. In the case of estimates of magnitude, our calling an object great is only made possible by reference to the standard with which it is compared. Kant may, therefore, regard the function of the standard here as tantamount to the 'concept of an end'. What would make this judgement of finality a case of the subjective mode is the fact that the standard involved is derived and applied informally 'by the eye alone' (i.e. without a definite mathematical concept in mind).[26] Yet even if we do 'have nothing in the way of a comparison present to . . . mind',[27] it would still follow that if, as Kant holds, all estimates of magnitude are comparative, then this logically presupposes the mediation of a concept, no matter how psychologically vague our awareness of it may be. Matters are further complicated by Kant's additional claim that

despite the standard of comparison being merely subjective, the claim of the judgement is nonetheless one to universal agreement; the judgements: 'That man is beautiful' and 'He is tall' do not purport to speak only for the judging Subject, but, like theoretical judgements, they demand the assent of every one.[28]

The fact that Kant mentions judgements of beauty and informal estimates of magnitude in the same breath here is surely significant. As we saw in Chapter 3, Kant takes himself to have

[25] Ibid. 96. Kant's use of the term '*a priori*' is puzzling here, in so far as while, say, the greatness of a virtue cannot be adequately presented in sensible experience, its greatness surely cannot be thought as independent of, or prior to, such empirical experience.

[26] Earlier on in § 26 (p. 95), Kant suggests that informal estimates of magnitude are subjectively final in 'reference to the power of judgement'. He does not, however, clarify this point. Indeed, one would have thought that subjective finality in relation to such an end would simply involve a harmony of imagination and understanding, i.e. would take the form of the pure judgement of taste.

[27] Ibid. 95.   [28] Ibid. 95.

established the universal validity of judgements of beauty without reference to definite concepts, by virtue of our justified assumption of a common sense. It may be that Kant has something like this in mind also in relation to informal estimates of magnitude—though it is difficult to see exactly how it would apply. I shall not, however, explore this problem further, since Kant's treatment of judgements of sublimity attempts (as we shall see) to articulate the universal validity of such judgements on somewhat different grounds.

In the central parts of § 25, Kant moves on to consider the nature of the feeling involved in sublimity—a topic which I will defer discussion of, in so far as it interrupts the logical progression of Kant's arguments. It is, indeed, not until the final part of § 25 that he is able to develop the implications of his initial claims that (i) greatness of magnitude can only be estimated comparatively, and (ii) it cannot be determined absolutely. This new development involves Kant linking these two claims to an elaboration of the other main contrast noted at the very start of the section—namely that which holds between, on the one hand, mere greatness and, on the other hand, the absolute greatness of the sublime. The transition to this second major stage of Kant's argument is effected by means of the following stratagem. Given that (by definition) the sublime is what is absolutely and beyond all comparison great, it must be found not in the things of nature but rather in our own ideas. Rather than give the reason for this immediately, Kant approaches it rather more circumspectly, through the introduction of a new definition:

the sublime is that in comparison with which all else is small. Here we readily see that nothing can be given in nature, no matter how great we judge it to be, which, regarded in some other relation, may not be degraded to the infinitely little, and nothing so small which in comparison with some smaller standard may not for our imagination be enlarged to the greatness of a world.[29]

On these terms, no phenomenal item is entitled to be called sublime because there is always some other phenomenal item or set of items in relation to which it can be regarded as small. Kant's new definition of the sublime as 'that in relation to which all else is small' is not particularly helpful. This is because, while

[29] *Judgement*, 97.

it ostensibly suggests that the difference between the sublime and other things is that even the vastest examples of the latter are smaller (i.e. have less extensive magnitude) than the former, Kant's real point is that what makes the sublime absolutely great is the fact that it pertains to our supersensible being (i.e. that which is beyond all questions of greatness of phenomenal magnitude). In this respect, we will remember that in Chapter 2 of this study I showed that on the basis of his Critical ethics Kant has good reason to reserve the term 'sublime' for our moral being alone, in so far as it is ontologically, axiologically, and cosmologically superior to any item or set of items in the phenomenal world. In § 25 in the *Critique of Judgement* Kant consolidates and supplements this position. Phenomenal items *qua* phenomenal items occupy determinate regions of space and time and their physical greatness is thereby relative to other such items. Our supersensible 'faculty' in contrast is beyond limitations of space and time even though it can bring about change in the spatio-temporal order.

It is at this point worth summarizing Kant's major claims in § 25 so far. First, by means of the contrast between estimating greatness and recognizing magnitude, Kant establishes that (i) the greatness of phenomenal items is always comparative, and (ii) it can never be determined absolutely. He then—by means of the further contrast between the comparative greatness of phenomenal items and the absolute greatness of the sublime— concludes that (iii) only our supersensible being can aptly be described as sublime. In the penultimate paragraph of § 25, Kant hints at a final crucial move. For it turns out that points (i), (ii), and conclusion (iii) do not simply serve to clarify the logic of the term sublime, but are, in effect, also psychological components in actual judgements of mathematical sublimity. That this is the case is hinted at in the following remarks.

precisely because there is a striving in our imagination towards progress *ad infinitum*, while reason demands absolute totality as a real idea, that same inability on the part of our faculty of the estimation of the magnitude of things of the world of sense to attain to this idea, is the awakening of a feeling of a supersensible faculty within us; and it is the use to which judgement naturally puts particular objects on behalf of this latter feeling and not the object of sense which is absolutely great.[30]

[30] Ibid. 97.

There are two features to note about this passage—one of which points ahead to Kant's crucial arguments about the psychological structure of judgements of sublimity in § 26, and the other of which introduces a problem. First, we must ask why imagination's inadequate striving to meet reason's demand for totality should be operative in informal estimations of magnitude. One would have thought that given some object we simply find the standard of comparison and make our estimate without further ado. However, what Kant has in mind here, I would suggest, hinges on claims (i) and (ii)—namely that greatness of magnitude is always comparative, and can never be determined absolutely. For—as becomes apparent in § 26—there are circumstances when, in our aesthetic estimates of magnitude, we are led to search out a measure (namely the idea of infinity as a whole) which, *if it could be grasped in imagination*, would enable us to determine magnitude in absolute terms. It is the very fact that imagination *cannot* grasp this idea of reason which evidences conclusion (iii)—the superiority of our supersensible rational being. This brings us to the problem opened up by the foregoing quotation. It centres on Kant's suggestion that it is the 'use' to which judgement puts formless objects in 'awakening' our feeling of a supersensible faculty which is 'absolutely great'. Matters seem further complicated by the fact that in the final paragraph of § 25 Kant informs us that *'The sublime is that,* [i.e. the idea of infinity as a whole] *the mere capacity of thinking which evidences a faculty of mind transcending every standard of sense.'*[31] At first sight, this all seems to suggest that Kant is proposing three different candidates for sublimity—our supersensible being itself, judgement's use of nature in awakening our feeling of this faculty, and finally the idea of infinity. However, in Kant's terms the sublimity of the two latter candidates can be construed as a reflection of the first's. As we have seen, in the Critical ethics Kant sees the sublimity of our moral being as arising fundamentally from the moral decision's 'independence of the mechanism of nature'. Nature itself plays only a negative role in so far as the sensible impulses of our natural being inhibit the workings of morality. But, as I showed in Chapter 3, Kant's fundamental strategy in the third *Critique* as a whole is to show

---

[31] *Judgement*, 98.

how the structure of the phenomenal world can be in harmony with morality in accordance with our assumption of the latter as the final end of Creation. Hence, given that even formless nature with its suggestion of infinity can (in ways which I will consider further on) evince the superiority of our supersensible moral being, the scope of this superiority is given a startling affirmation. It can employ the most physically overwhelming and chaotic aspects of nature *for its own ends*. On these terms, to experience the sublime via formless nature, is to experience a further aspect of the sublimity of our moral being.

In § 25, then, Kant sets out the basis of his approach to the mathematical sublime in a way that draws upon both his Critical ethics and his basic strategy in the third *Critique* as a whole. The main thrust of argument is aimed at clarifying the logic of the term sublime, but at the end of the section we also find a preliminary characterization of the psychological structure of judgements of mathematical sublimity. It is to the further elaboration of this structure that (as I shall now show) § 26 is principally addressed.

Kant begins § 26 with the observation that the estimation of magnitude through concepts of number is '*mathematical*', while an estimate made 'by the eye alone' is *aesthetic*. Kant's usage of the term 'aesthetic' here harks back to his definition of it at the start of the Analytic of the Beautiful. There we are told that an aesthetic judgement is 'one whose determining ground *cannot be other than subjective*'.[32] One presumes, therefore, that, because estimates of magnitude 'by the eye alone' do not involve a *definite* mathematical concept, they count thereby as subjectively determined and thence 'aesthetic'. Since I have already mentioned the problematic nature of this approach (in my discussion of the 'subjective finality' of informal estimates of magnitude) I shall move straight on to the complex relationship which Kant now sees as holding between mathematical and aesthetic estimates of magnitude. In relation to the former, we are told that

we can only get definite concepts of how great anything is by having recourse to numbers (or, at any rate, by getting approximate measurements by means of numerical series progressing *ad infinitum*), the unit being the measure.[33]

---

[32] Ibid. § 1, pp. 41–2.   [33] Ibid. § 26, p. 98.

Hence, the mathematical estimation of magnitude involves a relation between an object, a unit of measure, and a numerical series. Although Kant does not explicitly say so, this relation can be embodied in two different ways. On the one hand we can estimate how many times the unit of measure fits into the object, and, on the other hand, if the unit of measure is bigger than the object, we can estimate how many times the object fits into the measure. However, in whichever of these directions we proceed we arrive at the same problem. Kant expresses it as follows:

> But as the magnitude of the measure has to be assumed as known quantity, if to form an estimate of this, we must again have recourse to numbers involving another standard for their unit, and consequently must again procede mathematically, we can never arrive at a first or fundamental measure, and so cannot get any definite concept of a given magnitude. The estimation of the magnitude of the fundamental measure must, therefore, consist merely in the grasp we can get of it in intuition, and the use to which imagination can put this in presenting the numerical concepts: i.e. all estimation of the magnitude of objects of nature is in the last resort aesthetic.[34]

Kant's point here is that mathematical concepts provide us only with rules of progression in relation to measurement. But these can allow us to assign a definite magnitude to an object only if, at some point, they utilize a 'fundamental' measure which is taken as simply 'given' in intuition (i.e. comprehended 'by the eye' in 'aesthetic' terms). This is why Kant says that in the 'last resort' *all* estimates of magnitude are aesthetic. Kant's reasoning here has much to recommend it, in so far as having rules of multiplication or division or whatever is clearly not sufficient to determine an object's magnitude. We need in addition some given unit of measure, such as a metre or a mile, which we can multiply or divide by.

However, Kant's argument now takes a more difficult turn. We are told that

> for the mathematical estimation of magnitude there is, of course, no greatest possible . . . but for the aesthetic estimation there certainly is, and of it I say that where it is considered an absolute measure beyond which no greater is possible subjectively . . . it then conveys the idea of the sublime.[35]

[34] *Judgement*, § 26, p. 98.   [35] *Judgement*, 98–9.

As we have seen, in the passage immediately preceding this, Kant holds that, in order to form definite concepts of magnitude, we have to take certain measures as 'fundamental' (i.e. simply given in intuition). His point now is that once such a measure is provided we can, in principle, mathematically determine the magnitude of even the vastest objects—there is 'no greatest possible'. But in those aesthetic estimates which (as becomes clear further on in § 26) are directed towards vast formless objects, it is difficult even to find an appropriate measure. Indeed in our striving in this direction we are driven towards a measure which is fundamental in the sense of being 'absolute'. By 'absolute' here, Kant has two things in mind. First, whereas the use of mathematical concepts allows magnitude to be estimated only in relative terms, the use of an absolute measure 'presents magnitude absolutely, so far as the mind can grasp it in an intuition'.[36] The qualifying clause here is crucial and leads us to Kant's second point. For while this absolute measure *could* enable us to determine magnitude absolutely *if* we could grasp it in an intuition, the fact is that we *cannot* do so. From the viewpoint of our subjective (i.e. sensible) existence, it is absolute in the sense of being a 'greatest possible' which, no matter how hard we strive, we cannot grasp with any completeness. This is hardly surprising since much later on in § 26 Kant informs us that 'the proper unchangeable fundamental measure of nature is its absolute whole, which with it, regarded as phenomenon means infinity comprehended'.[37]

However, while we cannot grasp infinity in sensible intuition, we can (under conditions which I will consider a little further on) at least think it as an idea of reason, thereby evidencing the superiority of our rational over our sensible being. We are thus led to the 'idea of the sublime'.

Having thus set out the basic framework of his theory in this first stage of argument in § 26, Kant now goes on to elaborate some of its details. This next stage begins with what I shall call the 'watershed' passage of § 26. Here Kant describes what is actually involved in finding or attempting to find a measure for use in estimates of magnitude. First,

---

[36] Ibid. 99.
[37] Ibid. 104.

To take in a quantum intuitively in the imagination so as to be able to use it as a measure, or unit for estimating magnitude by numbers, involves two operations of this faculty: apprehension . . . and comprehension . . . Apprehension presents no difficulty: for this process can be carried on ad infinitum: but with the advance of apprehension comprehension becomes more difficult at every step, and this is the aesthetically greatest fundamental measure for the estimate of magnitude. For if the apprehension has reached a point beyond which the representations of sensuous intuition in the case of the parts first apprehended begin to disappear from the imagination as this advances to the apprehension of yet others, as much, then, is lost at one end as is gained at the other, and for comprehension we get a maximum which the imagination cannot exceed.[38]

The terms 'apprehension' and 'comprehension' here function in effect as an equivalent to the first two elements in the first *Critique*'s 'threefold synthesis of imagination'. In the 'synthesis of apprehension' (i.e. what Kant now calls simply 'apprehension') a manifold of sensible intuitions is 'run through, and held together'.[39] In the 'synthesis of reproduction in imagination' (or 'comprehension', as Kant now styles it) past sensible intuitions are held in memory alongside current ones, thus enabling the mind to grasp 'whole series of perceptions'.[40] Yet what makes the above passage from the third *Critique* so acutely problematic is Kant's ambiguity as to its scope. The fact that I have explained it by reference to the first *Critique*'s account of what is required in order to receive and comprehend *any* whole of sensible intuitions suggests that the process which Kant describes in § 26 of the third *Critique* can be operative in our very attempts even to *perceive* all the parts of a vast object as a totality, let alone estimate the magnitude of its vastness. And Kant follows up the passage in question with examples which (as I shall show below) illustrate just this point. Even so, we must remember that at the start of the passage Kant himself says that what he is describing is the process involved in finding a measure whereby the greatness of an object's magnitude can be estimated; and this would provide a logical follow on to his immediately preceding stage of argument concerning the absolute or (as Kant sometimes puts it) 'fundamental aesthetic' measure. Given, therefore, that this latter

[38] *Judgement*, 99.
[39] *Pure Reason*, A99, p. 131.   [40] Ibid. A121, p. 144.

course constitutes Kant's main thrust of argument so far in § 26, I will follow the way he develops it before looking at the alternative approach opened up by the 'watershed passage'.

As it happens, it is in the second part of § 26 that Kant develops his main thrust of argument most completely. He begins by reiterating at some length that mathematical estimates of magnitude are 'objectively final' and therefore not aesthetically pleasing. Indeed, in such mathematical estimates,

understanding is as well served and as satisfied whether imagination selects for the unit a magnitude which can be taken in at a glance e.g. a foot, or a perch, or else a German mile, or even the earth's diameter.[41]

However, if, in contrast, we attempt to determine magnitude by reference to the 'fundamental aesthetic measure', imagination is tested to the full. Kant describes this attempt in the following terms.

The mind . . . hearkens now to the voice of reason, which for all given magnitudes . . . requires totality, and consequently comprehension in *one* intuition, and which calls for a *presentation* answering to all the above members of a progressively increasing numerical series, and does not exempt even the infinite . . . from this requirement but rather renders it inevitable for us to regard this infinite . . . as completely given (i.e. given in its totality).[42]

As I interpret him here, Kant is saying that in the case of vast formless objects reason demands that we estimate their magnitude in relation to a unit of measure provided by a single intuition. In order to satisfy this demand the imagination will at first try out easily comprehended measures such as a foot or a perch, but is then driven to find larger units as a measure for them, and then still larger units as a measure for these, and so on and so on, until it arrives at infinity itself as the only appropriate measure. But by this time imagination is simply overwhelmed. It is driven by reason to comprehend infinity in a single intuition, but cannot even begin to do so. This, according to Kant, shows that our very capacity to frame the idea of infinity as a totality in rational terms 'indicates a faculty of mind transcending every standard of sense'.[43]

---

[41] *Judgement*, 102.
[42] Ibid. 102. Cf. the final paragraph of § 26 (ibid. 105).
[43] Ibid. 102.

Indeed,

the mere ability to think the given infinity [i.e. the idea of infinity comprehended as a totality] without contradiction is something that requires the presence in the human mind of a faculty that is itself supersensible. For it is only through this faculty and its idea of a noumenon, which latter . . . is yet introduced as a substrate underlying the intuition of the world as mere phenomenon, that the infinite of the world of sense in the pure intellectual estimation of magnitude, is *completely* comprehended *under* a concept.[44]

Kant's points here bring, I would suggest, two somewhat different considerations to bear. First, to think infinity as a whole presupposes (as we have seen) the capacity for theoretical reason itself, that is, a 'faculty' which (in the terms of Kant's broader philosophical position) is a supersensible one. However, Kant's other points raise a crucial interpretative issue. In the Transcendental Dialectic of the first *Critique* we are told that

I cannot say . . . that the world is *infinite* in space, or regards past time. Any such concept of magnitude, as being that of a given infinitude is empirically impossible, and, therefore, in reference to the world as an object of the senses, also absolutely impossible.[45]

Given this position, why is it that in § 26 of the third *Critique* Kant does hold that 'given infinity' can be 'thought without contradiction'? The key to this is hinted at in another passage in the Transcendental Dialectic of the first *Critique*. There Kant remarks that

reason through its demand for the unconditioned must remain in conflict with itself, or this unconditioned must be posited outside the series [of regressions of phenomenal appearances] in the intelligible [i.e. supersensible domain].[46]

While in the first *Critique* Kant's attempts to establish the possibility of a priori knowledge involve a crucial distinction between the phenomenal and the supersensible, we have seen that the Postulates of Pure Practical Reason in the second *Critique* are regarded by him as offering the best reasons for believing in the existence of a supersensible substrate to the

---

[44] *Judgement*, 103.
[45] *Pure Reason*, A520/B548, p. 457. Cf. *Judgement*, § 26, p. 104.
[46] *Pure Reason*, A564/B592, p. 482.

phenomenal world. This explains Kant's position in § 26 of the third *Critique* and, indeed, in his general discussion of the mathematical sublime. We *can* coherently think the idea of 'given infinity' *if* we regard the phenomenal world as limited or conditioned by that supersensible realm which the Critical ethics gives us best reason to believe in. The idea of 'infinity as a whole' or comprehended as a totality is coherent if we regard the supersensible substrate as serving, as it were, to circumscribe the world. Hence, our very capacity coherently to think the idea of infinity as a whole is not only a *manifestation* of our rational supersensible being, but also entails *reference* to the supersensible as part of the content of the idea itself. This means that imagination's inadequacy in the attempt to find an absolute measure both manifests the superiority of the supersensible and serves to draw our attention to the idea of it.

The final step in Kant's major thrust of reasoning consists in drawing out the implications of these arguments. In particular, he suggests that imagination's inadequacy in the aesthetic estimate of a vast object's magnitude is in 'subjective accord' with reason. This point is stated most completely in a passage in § 27. Here we are told that

The feeling of the sublime is . . . at once a feeling of displeasure, arising from the inadequacy of imagination in the aesthetic estimation of magnitude to attain to its estimation by reason, and a simultaneously awakened pleasure, arising from this very judgement of the inadequacy of sense being in accord with ideas of reason, so far as the effort to attain to these is for us a law.[47]

Kant's point here is that—as the framework of the Critical philosophy as a whole shows—what defines human beings is our rational vocation, that is our capacity to think or act independently of natural causality and in accordance with 'our own idea of laws'. The pursuit of reason is a law for us, in so far as we are true to our ultimate vocation. In the attempt to comprehend infinity as an absolute measure imagination's inadequacy is first experienced as a frustration, but then gives way to a pleasure arising from our awareness that this inadequacy in relation to an idea of reason exemplifies our ultimate vocation—to make reason triumph over sensibility. We become

[47] *Judgement*, § 27, p. 106.

aware that we are beings with capacities that transcend the limitations of our finite phenomenal existence. It is, however, important to be clear about the sense in which this complex experience of the sublime is in 'harmony' or 'accord' with the law of our rational vocation. For example, while in such an experience it is an idea of *theoretical* reason (i.e. infinity) which overwhelms imagination, this does not mean that the judgement of sublimity is thereby conducive to the exercise of theoretical reason. Rather (returning now to § 26) the mind 'feels itself empowered to pass beyond the narrow confines of sensibility'.[48] Indeed a judgement of the sublime is able 'to induce a temper of mind conformable to that which the influence of definite (practical) [i.e. moral] ideas would produce upon feeling, and in common accord with it'.[49] On these terms the judgement of sublimity is in accord or harmony with the law of our rational vocation because it produces a state of feeling analogous to the effect of that produced by morality, and this (Kant presumes) will make it *conducive* to morality. In the sublime, therefore, the faculties of imagination and reason are engaged in a relation which is *subjectively final* in relation to reason's highest end—our moral existence.

Let me now provide a brief summary of Kant's complex argument. (i) In our encounter with vast formless objects, we are led to estimate the greatness of their magnitude by reference to the absolute measure—namely infinity as a whole. (ii) Yet in searching out this fundamental aesthetic measure imagination is led into a regress that quickly overwhelms its powers of comprehension. It is totally unable to present the measure in terms of the single intuition which reason demands. (iii) Despite this, the felt frustration of imagination's inadequacy gives way to a feeling of pleasure at the fact that—in accordance with our ultimate vocation—reason has triumphed over sensibility and shown, thereby, that we have a faculty which transcends the limitations of our phenomenal being. (iv) Since this experience is analogous to the effect produced by morality, it will indirectly promote that end. (v) Hence: just as, in judgements of taste, imagination and understanding are subjectively final in relation to cognition generally, so too in judgements of sublimity the

---

[48] *Judgement*, § 26, p. 103.   [49] Ibid. 104.

faculties of imagination and theoretical reason are final in relation to reason's highest end—morality itself.

This completes my exposition of the main, rather baroque, direction of argument in Kant's account of the mathematical sublime. I shall defer consideration of the many critical questions it raises until after my exposition of the Dynamical sublime in the next chapter of this study.

Before that, however, there are still several tasks outstanding. The first of these pertains to an alternative and rather more austere formulation of the mathematical sublime which I suggested was opened up by the 'watershed' passage of § 26. Since there are several other hints of this alternative approach to be found in §§ 26 and 27, I shall bring these together before considering the crucial passage. Let us begin with the following observations from § 26. Kant remarks that for *any* given magnitude '—even for those which can never be completely apprehended, though (in sensuous representation) estimated as completely given—[reason] requires totality, and consequently comprehension in *one* intuition'.[50] Again, at the start of § 27, we are told that 'the idea of the comprehension of any phenomenon whatever, that may be given us, in a whole of intuition, is an idea imposed on us by a law of reason'.[51] The way Kant goes on to develop both these passages is by relating them to that search for an adequate presentation of infinity as a whole which is required as a measure in relation to vast objects. But we must attend closely to Kant's wording. I would suggest that it strongly implies that what reason demands is the comprehension of the *phenomenal totality* of any given magnitude in a single whole of intuition—that is, irrespective of whether or not it is to be used as a measure in the estimation of magnitude. By 'phenomenal totality' here, I mean all the different major parts or aspects which an object can present to perception—including those which, due to its or our location, are not presently accessible. In the case of small objects we can easily form an image which comprehends all their various phenomenal aspects. For example, on seeing a tobacco tin, it is easy to imagine all those parts of it which are hidden from our present viewpoint. Again, if we imagine an object which is not immediately present—such as a

---

[50] Ibid. 102.
[51] Ibid. § 27, p. 105.

house we have visited—we can easily form a sense of its phenomenal totality by recalling all its different rooms, stairways, and walls, etc. In these cases we have an image (or 'single whole of intuition' in Kant's terms) which comprehends the object's phenomenal totality *to the degree that none of its major parts are beyond our powers of imaginative recall or projection*. Yet the crucial point is that, the larger the object becomes, the more difficult is the comprehension of all its phenomenal parts as a totality. It is at this point that the 'watershed' passage of § 26 becomes relevant. There Kant describes the process of apprehension and comprehension. Specifically, we are told that

if the apprehension [of parts of a manifold] has reached a point beyond which the representations of sensuous intuition in the case of the parts first apprehended begin to disappear from the imagination as this advances to the apprehension of yet others, as much, then, is lost at one end as is gained at the other, and for comprehension we get a maximum which the imagination cannot exceed.[52]

Kant's point is that, in trying to comprehend some object in a single whole of intuition, the more parts we apprehend the more difficult this task proves. Indeed, imagination soon reaches its maximum of comprehension. *My* point, though, is that, while Kant discusses this process only in relation to the attempt to present infinity as an absolute measure, it must also apply in relation to our attempts to grasp the phenomenal totality of *any* object in a single whole of intuition. With large objects this will be particularly difficult. We will not be able to comprehend them in terms of an image which leaves no major aspect or part of the object beyond imaginative recall or projection. But despite this we will at least be able to comprehend the object as forming a totality in *rational* terms; and this, in a Kantian framework, serves to display the superiority of our rational over our sensible being.

One putative objection to this approach would be to cite a point noted earlier, namely Kant's account in § 27 of how we can immediately comprehend vast magnitudes through a 'subjective movement' of the imagination which suspends the time-series involved in apprehension. This (so the objection would go) shows that imagination can, in fact, meet reason's demand for

[52] *Judgement*, § 26, p. 99.

totality at least in relation to the comprehension of vast objects (though not of course in relation to the absolute measure). However, while this abbreviated mode of comprehension may enable imagination to cope with reason's demands in a practical everyday sense, it cannot wholly satisfy them. This is because, in Kant's terms, reason is a faculty which demands unconditional completeness. Hence, the only whole of sensible intuition which could fully satisfy reason's demand for a *complete* grasp of an object's magnitude would be one which encompassed its phenomenal totality in the sense noted earlier. Since imagination cannot frame such an intuition of vast objects, its failure in this respect accordingly manifests the superiority of reason.

What I am arguing, then, is that, in the terms of Kant's theory, reason's superiority to imagination can be embodied in the very attempt to even perceptually comprehend a large object. There is no need at all to invoke the process of searching out a fundamental measure. Interestingly, Kant follows up the 'watershed' passage by illustrating it with examples that seem to embody this very possibility (i.e. an austere route to the mathematical sublime). Kant introduces these by saying that his account of 'apprehension' and 'comprehension' (in the 'watershed' passage) 'explains' Savary's observation that

in order to get the full emotional effect of the size of the Pyramids we must avoid coming too near just as much as remaining too far away. For in the latter case the representation of the apprehended parts (the tiers of stones) is but obscure, and produces no effect upon the aesthetic judgement of the Subject. In the former, however, it takes the eye some time to complete the apprehension from the base to the summit; but in the interval the first tiers always in part disappear before the imagination has taken in the last, and so the comprehension is never complete.[53]

It must be admitted that this passage is puzzling. For what Kant is actually doing is *disproving* Savary's claim that to experience the 'full emotional effect' of the Pyramids we must see them from neither too far away nor too near. Kant shows, rather, that if we view them from close proximity our capacity for comprehension is soon overwhelmed. It is *this* which leads us to the full emotional affect. This is made clear by the example which is offered immediately after the foregoing. As Kant puts it,

[53] Ibid. 99–100.

The same explanation may also sufficiently account for the bewilderment, or sort of perplexity, which, as is said, seizes the visitor on first entering St Peter's in Rome. For here a feeling comes home to him of the inadequacy of his imagination for presenting the idea of a whole within which that imagination attains its maximum, and, in its fruitless efforts to extend this limit, recoils upon itself, but in so doing succumbs to an emotional delight.[54]

Again (as we shall see in more detail in Chapter 6) it is odd that Kant should choose examples of human artifice to illustrate the experience of the sublime. However, the point of capital importance is that Kant here articulates it without any reference to searching out infinity as a whole in order to serve as an absolute measure. Instead, in the above examples imagination simply proves inadequate to reason's demand that it present the object's phenomenal totality in a single whole of intuition. This in itself evidences the superiority of our rational and supersensible being, and brings about, therefore, the emotional delight of the sublime.

I am arguing that Kant's account of the mathematical sublime involves the interweaving of two rather different lines of argument. On the one hand there is the major—rather baroque—thesis about vast objects leading us to search out infinity in order to provide a measure for the estimation of their magnitude; and on the other hand there is the minor, more austere account which arrives at the sublime through imagination's inadequacy to satisfy reason's idea of the object as a whole (i.e. present an intuition corresponding to the idea of its phenomenal totality). The extraordinary complexity of Kant's theory is in part due to the fact that he does not clearly articulate that he *is* using two different approaches. That Kant does not do this is particularly unfortunate in that his major baroque thesis seems both phenomenologically counter-intuitive and philosophically superfluous. If we attempt to gauge the size of vast objects does this necessarily point us in the direction of searching out ever larger measures in order to estimate their vastness? Indeed, while Kant's explanation of the experience of the sublime hinges upon reason's demands in relation to sensibility, these demands are, nevertheless, sufficiently accounted for in the austere thesis. There is no reason why

---

[54] *Judgement*, § 26, p. 100.

infinity *must* play a role here. It may be that on occasion vast objects do suggest the idea of infinity to us, but even this might be explained more economically than in terms of the baroque thesis. In § 26, for example, Kant himself suggests that 'Nature . . . is sublime in such of its phenomena as in their intuition convey the idea of their infinity.'[55] This would indicate that, sometimes, the way a particular vast object swamps our imagination makes the object itself *seem* infinite. But 'seeming' infinite does not necessarily involve any complex process of the sort Kant describes. One could argue, rather, that our difficulty in comprehending a vast object in imagination is, at the level of judgement, *structurally similar* to the difficulty we would have in likewise comprehending the idea of infinity as a whole. Hence, the existence of such a structural analogy will sometimes make the former suggestive or 'symbolic' of the latter in broadly the same way, as Kant regards beauty as being symbolic of morality. On these terms, the suggestion of infinity would be regarded as a by-product of the way the object overwhelms the senses, that is as something which will intensify or enhance the experience of the sublime, rather than something which is necessarily involved in its production.

These points suggest that, if Kant had organized his exposition around the austere approach, he would not only have bypassed some difficulties but would still have been able—in the terms of his broader aesthetic theory—to find a role (albeit diminished) for the idea of infinity. Why, then, does Kant not develop his austere theory beyond a few tentative probings? Why is it that infinity shoulders so much of the burden of Kant's arguments? There are three broad answers to this. First, as it stands, there is nothing distinctively mathematical about the austere thesis since it involves neither numerical rules nor searching out comparative measures to estimate magnitude. Hence, I would suggest that Kant uses the idea of infinity as a whole construed as an absolute measure in order to emphasize the mathematical (i.e. bolster his fundamental architechtonic distinction between mathematical and dynamic). The second reason for the primacy of infinity in Kant's theory pertains to his relation with preceding theorists of the sublime. In the eighteenth century the link

---

[55] *Judgement*, § 26, p. 103. Again, Kant is being inconsistent here in describing nature itself as sublime.

between the experience of the sublime, infinity, and the incapacity of certain mental faculties played a crucial role in such theories. Addison, for example, observes that

The understanding . . . opens an infinite space on every side of us, but the imagination, after a few faint efforts, is immediately at a stand, and finds herself swallowed up in the immensity of the void that surrounds it; our reason can pursue a particle of matter through an infinite variety of divisions but the fancy soon loses sight of it . . . the object is too big for our capacity when we would comprehend the circumference of a world, and dwindles into nothing when we endeavour after the idea of an atom.[56]

The affinity between this passage and Kant's theory is quite remarkable. In particular, not only do Addison and Kant share the same terminology of 'understanding', 'imagination', and 'reason', but they seem, indeed to be assigning broadly the same roles to them. Even allowing for this, Kant is not just inheriting aspects of Addison's theory. The notion of infinity also has (as I pointed out earlier) a special significance for Kant. In the first *Critique*, he argues that the idea of infinity-as-a-whole is only coherent if we suppose the existence of a supersensible substrate to nature. Hence, by emphasizing the role of infinity in his theory of the sublime Kant is not only relating his work to an established tradition but is doing so by means of a concept which points directly to one of the central notions in his overall philosophical position (i.e. the noumenal realm).

The third reason for Kant's emphasis on infinity as an absolute measure is one which assumes especial importance in relation to the very possibility of the sublime as an aesthetic concept. I shall, therefore, defer discussion of it until my critical review of Kant's theory as a whole—which will be offered in Section III of the next chapter of this study. Before proceeding to that chapter, however, I want finally to look at an interesting hiatus in Kant's theory of the mathematical sublime. This consists in the status to be assigned to the infinitely tiny. Kant dismisses this notion summarily and suggests that we couple 'a kind of contempt with what we call infinitely small'.[57] The questions which this raises are those of why Kant's dismissal is so summary, and whether it

---

[56] Joseph Addison, *Critical Essays from 'The Spectator'*, ed. Donald Bond (Clarendon Press: Oxford, 1970), essay no. 420, p. 204.
[57] *Judgement*, § 25, p. 96.

is justified. In this respect it might be claimed that we can surely take some phenomenal object and imagine it being divided into smaller and smaller units in the direction of infinity. Does not William Blake talk of seeing 'infinity in a grain of sand'? To be consistent, Kant's response to this would probably take the following form. We can indeed imagine a grain of sand being reduced to smaller and smaller units, but a limit to our imaginings is soon reached. We may envisage the grain-parts in terms of microscopic particles and then atoms; but what, phenomenally speaking, are these entities like? The problem is here that, whereas we have direct or telescopic acquaintance with the sun, stars, and other heavenly bodies, and can imagine these multiplied towards infinity, we have no similar intuitions of sub-microscopic particles. This means that, while in relation to the vast spaces of the macroscopic world imagination has, as it were, something to grasp at, in the sub-microscopic sphere we quickly arrive at the utterly unknown. So far from being tested to its utmost, imagination here, as Addison aptly puts it, 'dwindles into nothing'. Although it is, I would suggest, something like these points which underpins Kant's summary dismissal of the infinitely small in relation to the mathematical sublime, his dismissal is, nevertheless, still not justified. In this respect it is interesting that the image of seeing infinity in a grain of sand derives from a work of poetry. This would suggest that, while we do not have sensible intuitions of the sub-microscopic sphere, we can still creatively imagine such intuitions in terms of analogies, images, and metaphors taken from the realm of macroscopic space and its contents. For example, at the end of the science-fiction film *The Incredible Shrinking Man* (1957) the film's central character descends into the abyss of the microscopic and beyond. This descent is evoked by a sequence of images connoting movement through endless chambers inhabited by unfamiliar organic or inorganic entities. Of course, we have no way of knowing whether the micro-world would really look like this, but the point is that we can at least imagine it in such terms. Imagination could be overwhelmed in even trying to comprehend the possible appearances of the micro-world, and art can be particularly efficacious in stimulating us in this direction.

Having completed my exposition of Kant's theory of the mathematical sublime, I shall now consider his account of the Dynamic mode.

5

From the Dynamical Mode of Sublimity to the Deduction, and an Overall Critical Review

I

After the labyrinthine intricacies of the Mathematical mode, Kant's discussion of the dynamical sublime comes as something of a relief, in so far as it contains one of the clearest progressions of argument in any one section of the third *Critique*. First Kant defines 'might' as that which is superior to great hindrances, and which is to be regarded as having 'dominion' if those hindrances are themselves mighty. This definition leads, in turn, to the claim that, if we judge aesthetically that nature is might that has no dominion over us, then we are experiencing the dynamically sublime. The basis of such judgements is as follows.

If we are to estimate nature as dynamically sublime, it must be represented as a source of fear (though the converse, that every object that is a source of fear is, in our aesthetic judgement, sublime, does not hold). For in forming an aesthetic estimate (no concept being present) the superiority to hindrances can only be estimated according to the greatness of the resistance. Now that which we strive to resist is an evil, and, if we do not find our powers commensurate to the task, an object of fear.[1]

Kant's point here is that to judge an object as possessing might is simply to make a logical judgement on the basis of concepts. However, if our judgement is to be aesthetic (i.e. one whose determining ground is subjective) then our estimation of the object as mighty must be determined by our affective response to it, that is by the amount of fear it would engender in our futile efforts to resist its might.[2]

[1] Kant, *Judgement*, 109–10.
[2] Presumably, if we could resist it, it would be an object of pleasure.

This leads to Kant's most fundamental distinction in § 28. We are told that

> we may look upon an object as *fearful*, and yet not be afraid *of* it, if, that is, our estimate takes the form of our simply *picturing to ourselves* the case of our wishing to offer some resistance to it, and recognising that all such resistance would be quite futile.[3]

Hence, while, for example, a good man is not in an actual state of fear before God, he can, nevertheless, imagine a situation where he *would* be in such a state through some futile attempt to resist the Divine Will. He recognizes God as a potential object of occurrent fear.

On these terms, the might of nature is aesthetically disclosed in two ways—through actual, or through imagined, fear. In relation to the former, Kant points out that a person in actual fear is no more able to judge the sublime than someone who is beset by inclination and appetite is able to judge the beautiful. Indeed, in the case of actual fear, we flee from the object which is causing us so much distress. While the cessation of such actual fear gives rise to a state of joy, it also has two negative consequences: (i) we resolve never to put ourselves in such a dangerous situation again, and (ii) we find it distressing even to recall the event. These points are of some importance, since through them Kant is, I think, inviting a comparison at the expense of Burke.[4] Burke holds that our pleasure in the sublime arises from the moderation of actual pain or terror, achieved through (in the case of pain) the weak *effect* of the causal stimulus (e.g. large objects) and in the latter case through the distance between us and the object of terror. However, Kant's implicit point is that, if judgements of sublimity involved genuine and actual states of pain and terror, then, no matter how pleasurable the moderation or cessation of such states might be, we would not want to go through the experience again. But since we clearly do put ourselves in positions where objects already found sublime can be encountered again, and since indeed we do recall such situations with pleasure, then a Burkean cessation-of-terror explanation of sublimity will obviously not be adequate.

[3] *Judgement*, 110.
[4] See esp. Part I, Sections III, VII, and XVIII, of Burke's *A Philosophical Inquiry into the Origin of Our Ideas of the Sublime and the Beautiful*, ed. John Boulton (Routledge & Kegan Paul: London, 1958).

Where Kant does agree with Burke, though, is in the claim which follows on from this: that to experience the dynamically sublime we must be in a position of safety. In this respect, we are told that

the boundless ocean rising with rebellious force, the high waterfall of some mighty river, and the like, make our power of resistance of trifling moment in comparison with their might. But, provided our own position is secure, their aspect is all the more attractive for its fearfulness.[5]

The question of why this fearfulness is found attractive is considered at some length in the central portion of § 28. After having repeated a summary of his account of the mathematical sublime, Kant declares that

in just the same way the irresistibility of the might of nature forces upon us the recognition of our physical helplessness as beings of nature, but at the same time reveals a faculty of estimating ourselves as independent of nature, and discovers a pre-eminence above nature that is the foundation of a self-preservation of quite another kind . . . it challenges our power (one not of nature) to regard as small those things of which we are wont to be solicitous (worldly goods, health, and life), and hence to regard its might . . . as exercising over us and our personality no such rude dominion that we should bow down before it . . . Therefore nature is here called sublime merely because it raises the imagination to a presentation of those cases in which the mind can make itself sensible of the appropriate sublimity of the sphere of its own being, even above nature.[6]

As we saw in Chapter 4, while the mathematical sublime involves our capacity for *theoretical* reason, it is of indirect *moral* significance through disclosing the superiority of our supersensible being. In the case of the dynamical sublime, in contrast, an awareness of our moral existence plays a much more direct role. When beholding mighty natural objects from a position of safety, we recognize them to be fearful, but this challenges us to imagine situations where we would remain unflinching and courageous, even in the face of possible destruction by the mighty object. Kant arrives at this view by wedding an assumption about human responses to his earlier implicit objections to Burke. The assumption consists in the fact

[5] *Judgement*, 110–11.   [6] Ibid. 111.

that, faced with inevitable destruction by a mighty natural object, we can respond in two different ways. On the one hand, we can simply be overwhelmed by fears pertaining to our physical well-being and safety. This would be to respond as if we were sensuous finite beings alone, and entirely subject to determination by natural causality. On the other hand, we can, against our natural inclinations, transcend fear and face destruction courageously—thus acting on principles of moral conduct which testify to our true vocation as rational supersensible beings. Now since (as Kant's earlier arguments show) our pleasure in the sublime is not explicable in terms of the moderation of pain or terror, we require, in consequence, an alternative analysis of how the fearful character of the mighty natural object is turned to positive account. This is exactly what is provided by the second element in Kant's assumption. Our pleasure in the destructive object is explicable through its leading us to imagine a situation where, through our courageous moral bearing, we refute its (and thereby nature's) claim to dominion over us.

This completes my exposition of Kant's theory of the dynamical sublime. However, before considering the three putative objections which Kant raises and dismisses in relation to his theory, I want to look at an alternative reading of the central argument of § 28 (i.e. the claim that in judgements of the sublime we affirm, through moral bearing, the superiority of the rational, supersensible self). This alternative is found in a paper by William Hund, where it is claimed that

Although Kant did not explicitly state that this 'self-preservation of quite another kind' [included in the passage quoted earlier] is the immortality of the soul and not merely our moral and intellectual superiority over the brute forces of nature, I think that the context demands this interpretation. For if nature could kill the soul as well as the life of the body, then nature would have dominion over us. But since Kant held that nature has no dominion over us, then it follows that it is because nature cannot kill our soul.[7]

The problem with this interpretation (and the way Hund develops it) is that it gives a misleading over-emphasis to the

---

[7] William B. Hund, 'The Sublime and God in Kant's *Critique of Judgement*', *Scholastic* (Spring 1983), 42–70. This reference, p. 60.

immortality of the soul. Hund talks, indeed, as though our moral being and the immortality of the soul are logically unconnected with one another, and that it is the latter alone which frustrates nature's claim to dominion over us. But Kant does not separate the two notions, in so far as for him the immortality of the soul is a 'postulate of pure practical reason'. In the second *Critique* he argues that

complete fitness of the will to the moral law is holiness, which is a perfection of which no rational being in the world of sense is at any time capable. But since it is required as practically necessary, it can be found only in an endless progress to that complete fitness; on principles of pure practical reason, it is necessary to assume such a practical progress as the real object of our will.

This infinite progress is possible, however, only under the presupposition of an infinitely enduring . . . personality of the same rational being.[8]

On these terms, while reason demands a perfect harmony of our intentions with the moral law, *in practice*—as sensuous finite beings—we never do achieve such congruence. However, the achievement of such a state must be possible, otherwise by demanding the impossible of us, reason would itself, paradoxically, be unreasonable. Hence, the only way such an achievement is possible is on the assumption that the soul is immortal, and can progress from lower to higher degrees of moral perfection. I do not propose to dwell on the many difficulties raised by this account; it is sufficient for my present purposes to point out that when, in relation to the dynamical sublime, Kant talks of us discovering 'a self-preservation' other than that which pertains to our natural being, he is talking fundamentally of our rational and moral being—from which the existence of an immortal soul can be inferred. The latter without the former would simply not be able to frustrate nature's claim to dominion over us. For example, suppose a man performs his moral duty simply on the grounds that he will be rewarded in the afterlife. Suppose also that, while witnessing an avalanche in the distance, he imagines himself facing destruction by it—but is made happy by the thought that in such a situation he will be going to his everlasting reward. Here, while the man's pleasure would be

[8] *Practical Reason*, 225–6.

grounded on the immortality of the soul, not only would this fail to involve an awareness of the superiority of our moral and rational being (as Kant demands, in order for the judgement to be sublime) but it would, indeed, be implicitly allowing nature to have dominion over that being. To do one's duty on the expectation of being rewarded by immortality is to make morality subservient to the natural end of the desire for everlasting happiness. I am suggesting, then, that, in respect of Kant's notion of the dynamical sublime, the immortality of the soul would only be relevant in so far as we were led to it through the moral recognition of our status as rational beings.

This digression aside, let me now consider the three putative objections to his theory which Kant himself considers in the latter half of § 28. First, given that in our experience of the dynamical sublime the fearful object is encountered from a position of safety, and there is no serious possibility of danger, might it not, therefore, be plausibly argued that 'there is just as little seriousness in the sublimity of our faculty of soul'? I would suggest that Kant's worry here hinges on the role played by imagination in the sublime. If the danger is only imaginary, then perhaps we are at best playful, and at worst insincere, in our appreciation of the soul's sublimity. As a retort to this, Kant remarks that in judgements of sublimity

the delight only concerns the *province* of our faculty disclosed in such a case, so far as this faculty has its root in our nature; notwithstanding that its development and exercise is left to ourselves and remains an obligation. Here indeed there is truth—no matter how conscious a man, when he stretches his reflection so far abroad, may be of his present helplessness.[9]

Kant's reasoning here suffers from great awkwardness of presentation, but comes down to the following points. Our pleasure in sublimity pertains to the rational faculty viewed as a 'province' (i.e. a supersensible capacity whose employment transcends mere determination by nature's causal laws). The moral exercise of this capacity is an obligation grounded upon personal responsibility. However, even when it is not being occurrently exercised, the *possibility* of such employment remains a deep-seated tendency in human nature. Hence, while

[9] *Judgement*, 112.

in a judgement of sublimity we are not in circumstances where we can actually perform our duty (i.e. we are, in effect, rendered 'helpless' to perform it), these circumstances do allow us, nevertheless, to imagine a possible situation where our supersensible capacity *could* be exercised. We would not be entertaining the playful or the insincere, but would be countenancing a 'true' and genuine possibility of behaviour, rooted in the most fundamental supersensible aspect of human nature. Our judgement would, therefore, be far from lacking in seriousness.

Kant also offers two other putative objections to his theory, which I shall consider in reverse order of their presentation. First, does not the account offered in § 28 conflict with the fact that nature's destructive might is often taken as a manifestation of God in his wrath and sublimity? Hence it would be ridiculous to imagine our own minds as superior to that which manifests his sublimity. Indeed, the only way in which one could give due respect to the Divine Being in such circumstances would be to adopt an attitude of utter and abject helplessness. In relation to this latter point, Kant admits that, while the abject attitude is a common feature of religious practice, there is far from being any necessary link between it and the recognition of God's sublimity. If we are in a state of fear at God's manifestation in nature, through being conscious that we have offended him, then our attitude will be one based on concern for our own safety, rather than one based on genuine reverence for God's sublimity. It is only the good man (with a disposition in harmony with God's will) who occupies, as it were, a position of spiritual safety, from whence the might of nature can be appreciated as a sign of divine sublimity.[10] It is this which distinguishes authentic religious experience from the mere dread and apprehension of superstition.

Kant offers one other putative objection to his own theory, namely that (as he puts it) 'This principle [i.e. that sublimity involves reference to our rational disposition of soul] has, doubtless the appearance of being too far-fetched and subtle, and so of lying beyond the reach of an aesthetic judgement.'[11]

---

[10] Hund mistakenly supposes that Kant is making this into a necessary condition for the appreciation of the dynamically sublime as such. The structure of Kant's argument as I have outlined it, though, clearly shows that Kant is *directly* linking this only to the appreciation of God's sublimity.

[11] *Judgement*, 112.

In reply to this, Kant claims that common experience shows that judgements of sublimity do, in fact, make reference to our supersensible capacity—even though we may not be conscious of it. For example, even in a civilized society there is always a special regard for those soldiers who, through their gentle and humane bearing, show that they have transcended the terrible fears inherent in their way of life. Moreover,

comparing the statesman and the general, men may argue as they please as to the pre-eminent respect which is due to either above the other, but the verdict of the aesthetic judgement is for the latter. War itself, provided it is conducted with order and a sacred respect for the rights of civilians, has something sublime about it, and gives nations that carry it on in such a manner a stamp of mind only the more sublime the more dangers to which they are exposed, and which they are able to meet with fortitude.[12]

Kant's reasoning here is as follows. To estimate the respective merits of soldiers and statesmen is generally a task for debate, and hinges upon objective considerations. Yet from the purely subjective (and thence aesthetic) standpoint of feeling, we find that soldiers, and indeed war itself, stir our feelings[13] far more than statesmen or peace, precisely because they involve human beings transcending the interests of their sensible being. Kant, however, needs to make a qualification here. In his *Anthropology from a Pragmatic Point of View* (1798), he considers the example of a tribe of American Indians whose custom, on being surrounded by their enemies, is to throw down their weapons and submit to massacre, rather than plead for mercy. This, Kant declares, 'seems to me merely a barbarian conceit: to preserve the honour of their tribe by not letting the enemy compel them to lament and groan as evidence of their submission'.[14] What Kant needs to emphasize in § 28 of the third *Critique*, therefore, is that soldiers and war are only sublime in so far as martial actions are engaged in from motives of universal moral duty, rather than personal aggrandizement or blind loyalty to specific social ensembles. Even allowing for this qualification, it may,

---

[12] Ibid. 112–13.

[13] One presumes that our feeling of reverence for them stimulates the imagination into schematizing all sorts of scenes of heroism.

[14] Kant, *Anthropology from a Pragmatic Point of View*, trans. Mary Gregor (Martinus Nijhoff: The Hague, 1974), Book III, 125.

nevertheless, still seem outrageous to regard something so terrible as war itself to be anything less than an unmitigated evil. But Kant offers another argument to justify his approach. It is found in § 22 of the Critique of Teleological Judgement. There we are told that

> if, on the part of men war is a thoughtless undertaking, being stirred up by unbridled passions, it is nevertheless a deep-seated, maybe far-seeing, attempt on the part of supreme wisdom, if not to found, yet to prepare the way for a rule of law governing the freedom of states, and thus bring about their unity in a system established on a moral basis.[15]

On these terms, perhaps the major reason why, for Kant, war can be regarded as sublime is that, in the ultimate analysis, it is conducive to the realization of the final end—morality.

While I shall review the general questions raised by Kant's exposition of the dynamical sublime further on in this chapter, it is worth considering one difficulty now. The examples of soldiers and war are meant to show how Kant's basic claim in § 28 (namely that dynamical sublimity involves reference to our supersensible capacity) is borne out by common experience. However, this stratagem is clearly unsuccessful, in so far as these particular examples are not instances of the dynamical sublime as Kant has defined it in § 28 (i.e. they do not involve us achieving awareness of our supersensible capacity through confrontation with some fearful natural object or phenomenon). What Kant is, *in effect*, doing through his examples of soldiery and warfare is setting out a subcategory of dynamic sublimity whose origin is to be found in our affective response to rationally significant *human deeds*. This category is developed further in § 29, as the latter half of a subsection entitled 'GENERAL REMARK UPON THE EXPOSITION OF AESTHETIC REflECTIVE JUDGEMENTS'. Here Kant suggests that affects are occurrent states of pleasure or displeasure which carry us away and render us momentarily unable to make rational decisions. Such affects are of two sorts; on the one hand, we have the 'languid' type (such as sentimentality), and, on the other hand, we have 'the STRENUOUS TYPE (such, that is, as excites the consciousness of our overcoming every resistance . . .)' . . . e.g. anger, even desperation (the *rage of forlorn hope* but not *faint-hearted* despair).[16]

---

[15] *Judgement*, Book II, § 22, p. 96.   [16] Ibid. Book II, § 29, p. 25.

These, and other such examples of the strenuous type—such as enthusiasm, and a sadness which leads us to seek isolation from all society—are regarded by Kant as 'aesthetically sublime'. His reason for describing them in such terms is that they lead us to an awareness of our transcendence of sensible being. Yet is this not acutely paradoxical, given the fact that Kant defines affect as something which leaves us momentarily unable to make rational decisions? I would suggest not; for while feelings might overwhelm us in a way that stops us from actually making rational decisions, the very fact that we are thus released may allow us scope for reflecting on the fact that we *can* make such decisions, and, indeed, for imagining further situations wherein our supersensible capacity *can* or (if we are angry or desperate over the thwarting of our moral projects) *could* have been employed. Hence, while affective states are 'contra-final' in relation to the occurrent employment of reason, they are subjectively final in relation to reason construed dispositionally (i.e. they disclose the power and possibilities of our rational being).

I have argued, then, that Kant offers us two varieties of the dynamic sublime. The first of these (outlined in § 28) arises from us imagining some object as fearful through its capacity to physically destroy us, but leads us, nevertheless, also to imagine ourselves resisting it through our moral resolve. The second variety (introduced in § 28, but discussed most fully in § 29) holds that we experience the sublime when some affect arises in circumstances that enable us to become more generally aware of our moral capacity and its possible employments. A crucial point to note is the contrasting role played by imagination here, in comparison with that which it plays in the mathematical sublime. In the case of the latter, it is imagination's inability to meet the demands of reason which is the source of a displeasure that discloses the superiority of our rational being. In the § 28 variety of the dynamic sublime, however, it is those things which we imagine (i.e. the object's fearfulness and a situation where we morally resist it) which are displeasurable and pleasurable respectively. There is nothing in either of these features that would stretch the imagination to its limits. It is the easiest thing in the world to imagine our fear in the face of impending destruction by an avalanche; likewise (especially if one is of a

Romantic disposition) it takes little effort to imagine oneself showing dignity and moral resolve in such a terrifying situation. In relation to the affective variety of the dynamic sublime, matters are slightly different. Here we have an *occurrent* affective state of either pleasure (as in 'enthusiasm') or displeasure (as in Kant's example of anger) which stimulates us into a general awareness of the possibilities of our moral being. Putting it broadly, then, in the dynamic sublime an imagined or actual affective state leads the imagination to envisage possibilities of moral action. This means that here imagination is in a harmonious and relatively free relation to reason, in much the same way as are those 'aesthetic ideas' discussed later on in the Analytic of the Sublime. I shall return to this analogy in due course.

Let me now consider two other general interpretative perspectives which have been offered on Kant's notion of the dynamic sublime. First, the interpretation which I have proposed is somewhat at odds with that of H. W. Cassirer. He claims that

It will be obvious that Kant's theory of the dynamically sublime agrees in every respect with his theory of the mathematically sublime. He states once more that the Idea of sublimity arises from the fact that in representing the object to ourselves we feel the pre-eminence of our rational nature over physical nature in its immeasurability, and he sets forth the view that it is our consciousness of the incapacity of our imagination which makes us feel this.[17]

Yet the passage from § 28 which Cassirer is referring to in the second sentence of this quotation is one where Kant is explicitly reiterating his account of the mathematical sublime. This is made clear by the phrasing (in the past tense):

In the immeasurableness of nature and the incompetence of our faculty for adopting a standard proportionate to the aesthetic estimation of its *realm*, we found our own limitation. But with this we also found in our rational faculty another non-sensuous standard, one which has infinity itself under it as unit, and in comparison with which everything in nature is small.[18]

---

[17] H. W. Cassirer, *A Commentary on Kant's Critique of Judgement* (Methuen & Co Ltd: London, 1970), 244.
[18] *Judgement*, § 28, p. 111.

Kant then goes on to suggest that the dynamic sublime reveals our rational faculty 'in just the same way'. He does not, however, suggest that this likeness extends to the role played by imagination. This being said, it is nevertheless interesting that, in § 29, Kant does make several remarks which seem to be in accord with Cassirer's interpretation. For example,

this idea of the supersensible . . . is awakened in us by an object the aesthetic estimating of which strains the imagination to its utmost, whether in respect of its extension (mathematical), or of its might over the mind (dynamical).[19]

This might seem to suggest two possibilities. Either, in § 28, Kant simply does not bring out the fact that the imagination is stretched in trying to comprehend the object's fearfulness; or else he has two different versions of his main category of dynamical sublimity. There is good reason to reject both possibilities. It will be remembered that Kant holds that in the mathematical sublime the object is referred to the faculty of cognition (i.e. theoretical reason), whereas in the dynamical sublime it is referred to the faculty of desire (i.e. practical reason). Given this fundamental distinction, one would naturally expect that, in the former, reason demonstrates its superiority over sensibility in the form of imagination, while in the latter, reason demonstrates its superiority to sensibility in the form of sensuous impulse. To suppose that both involved the triumph of reason over imagination would be in serious conflict with Kant's fundamental architechtonic dichotomy. But why, then, in § 29, does Kant talk as though the role of imagination is the same in both modes? The answer to this, I would suggest, is again architechtonic. In § 29, Kant is (for the most part) talking about the sublime in general terms, and seeking to show that judgements in both its modes lay claim to necessity on the same ground: the justified presupposition of moral feeling as common to all. Given this, one can explain Kant's talking as though both modes of sublimity involved imagination in the same way, as a misleading attempt to paper over differences. It is also likely that Kant described both modes of sublimity in terms of the mathematical version simply for the sake of brevity. I am claiming, in other words, that the

[19] Ibid. 120.

incongruities that appear in §29 are due to the demands of writing a section grounded on general considerations.

Let me finally consider some problems raised by Paul de Man in relation to the dynamical sublime. First, he suggests that Kant's justification for introducing the dynamic sublime as a category at all is problematic. As he puts it,

One can grant that it is methodologically as legitimate to evaluate the impact on us of the sublime, as pleasure or pain, in terms of quantity instead of, as is the case with beauty, in terms of quality. But, if this is indeed the case, why then can the analytics of the sublime not be closed off with the section on the mathematical sublime centered on quantity and number?[20]

De Man then suggests that Kant's justification of the dynamic sublime through reference to the faculty of desire also raises problems, not the least of which is that 'when we reach the section on the dynamic sublime we find something quite different from desire'.[21]

Let me deal with these 'difficulties' in turn. First, the reason why the impact of the sublime upon us is not completely analysable in mathematical terms as extension is because (as has been shown in the first *Critique*) manifolds of intuition can also be synthesized dynamically (i.e. in terms of concepts pertaining to the physical powers and effects of phenomena). Hence, if our capacity for comprehensive synthesis can be overwhelmed by extension, we can also expect it to be overwhelmable by dynamic power. Indeed, if Kant's theory is to be comprehensive, he could hardly *not* account for our response to overwhelming power, since it figures large in that self-preservatory approach to the sublime which is found in Addison and (especially) Burke. In relation to de Man's second objection—that desire does not actually feature in Kant's discussion of the dynamical sublime— de Man is simply betraying his ignorance of Kant's technical usage. Certainly there is nothing like desire in the sense in which it is normally understood, but, for Kant, the faculty of desire is 'a faculty which by means of its representations is the cause of the actuality of the objects of those representations'.[22] Now when, in

---

[20] Paul de Man, 'Phenomenality and Materiality in Kant', in Gary Schapiro and Alan Sica (eds.), *Hermeneutics: Questions and Prospects* (University of Massachusetts Press: Amherst, 1984), 125.

[21] Ibid. 126.   [22] Kant, *Judgement*, 16 n.

relation to the dynamical sublime, the object which we imagine as fearful leads us in turn to imagine ourselves as morally resisting it, we are representing a course of action which, as moral beings, we are capable of realizing (i.e. causing 'the actuality of'). Within the terms of his own philosophy, Kant is quite consistent in linking the dynamical sublime to the faculty of desire, since it is the employment of this faculty through the imagination which discloses the possibilities of our supersensible being.

II

As a conclusion to the largely expository and interpretative part of this study, I shall now consider Kant's account of the phenomenological structure of judgements of sublimity, and their epistemological status. In relation to the first of these questions, while there is relevant material in all the sections so far considered, Kant's account focuses specifically on § 27. This section basically elaborates the phenomenological structure which Kant has ascribed to judgements of mathematical sublimity. There is, however, no parallel chapter wherein the phenomenological structure of the dynamical mode is elaborated upon. Kant's reasoning here is based on the fact that, while the moral significance of the dynamic sublime is extremely manifest, his account of the mathematical mode in §§ 25 and 26 has given rather less emphasis to this crucial dimension. By following up the mathematical sublime with a deeper account of its phenomenology, therefore, Kant creates an opportunity to emphasize that mode of sublimity's moral aspect. This is manifest in the very way he begins § 27. We are told that 'The feeling of our incapacity to attain to an idea *that is a law for us*, is RESPECT.'[23]

Phenomenologically speaking, this feeling involves

displeasure, arising from the inadequacy of imagination in the aesthetic estimation of magnitude to attain to its estimation by reason, and a simultaneously awakened pleasure, arising from this very judgement of the inadequacy of the greatest faculty of sense being in accord with ideas of reason, so far as the effort to attain to these is for us a law.[24] .

<hr>

[23] Ibid. 105.   [24] Ibid. 106.

It will be remembered that, in relation to beauty, Kant holds that the relation of imagination and understanding is a state of harmonious accord that is subjectively final for cognition in general. But here we have a relation of two higher faculties, where one fails to meet the demands of the other. Kant sees imagination and reason's engagement, indeed, as harmonious by virtue of their very conflict.[25] His basic reason for this is that if we were to ground the relationship between imagination and reason on some harmonious reciprocity of them *qua* cognitive faculties alone, there would be no room for the involvement of a state of displeasure, and he would thus be unable either to assimilate Burke's theory or to characterize the feeling of the sublime in terms of 'respect'. However, the question arises as to why Kant feels himself entitled to use this distinctively moral notion in relation to the feeling of sublimity. This very question brings to light an interesting ambiguity in Kant's position. At one point in § 27, for example, we are told that the feeling of the sublime 'renders, as it were, intuitable the supremacy of our faculties on the rational side over the greatest faculty of sensibility'.[26] Here Kant presents his point economically. It is a sense of the superiority of our rational supersensible being which provides the pleasurable component in judgements of sublimity. Of course, this supersensible being is, in Kant's terms, a morally significant idea, but an explicit awareness of this fact does not play any direct role here.[27] What Kant assumes, rather, is that any overcoming of sensibility by reason (in the broad sense of that term) will be of moral significance in so far as it will lead us to take a pleasure in the fact that we are more than creatures of sensibility. This, in turn, will render us all the more liable to follow the precepts of moral reason. To have our sensibility determined by theoretical reason prepares the ground for its determination by morality. It is this which makes the feeling of the sublime subjectively final in relation to the 'higher ends of reason' and makes it count, thereby, as a variety of respect.

[25] Kant, *Judgement*, 107.
[26] Ibid. 106.
[27] Characteristically, Kant sometimes talks as though it does. In § 25, for example, he suggests that judgements of the sublime 'involve the consciousness of a subjective finality' (ibid. 96)—but if *knowing* that the feeling of the sublime was final in relation to morality was one of the grounds of our taking pleasure in it, this would be the most flagrant contradiction of its putatively aesthetic status.

Interestingly, Kant is ambiguous as to the nature of the 'mental movement' involved in this feeling. As we have seen, he describes the states of pleasure and displeasure as 'simultaneous'. Elsewhere in § 27, however, we are told that 'This movement, especially in its inception, may be compared with a vibration, i.e. with a rapidly alternating repulsion and attraction produced by one and the same object.'[28]

Earlier still in the third *Critique*, Kant observes that 'the feeling of the sublime is a pleasure that only arises indirectly, being brought about by the feeling of a momentary check to the vital forces followed at once by a discharge all the more powerful'.[29]

Why, then, does Kant offer these different accounts of the mental movement involved in sublimity? In relation to this very problem, Paul Guyer has proposed two explanations. First, Kant thought that, while the feeling of the sublime is, phenomenologically speaking, a single but a complex one, it must, nevertheless, be theoretically analysable in Humean terms as a succession of distinct sensations. Second, Kant may also have been unsure as to *how far* judgements of sublimity involve 'pre-reflective' psychological processes that can only be recognized through feelings of pleasure and displeasure. If such processes are wholly 'pre-reflective', then 'there would be no obvious reason why both sorts of feelings should not become conscious simultaneously'.[30]

However, Guyer suggests that in § 27 Kant may have moved from this position to that of a succession of feelings because

he might have recognised that while it is at least plausible to think of the striving of the imagination . . . as actually manifesting itself to awareness only in a feeling of failure, the *interpretation* of the significance of this interpretation . . . would seem to require a conscious reflection in conceptual terms. Recognising this, Kant might have been tempted tacitly to interpose a judgement between the feeling of frustration and the feeling of pleasure . . . and thus to introduce a temporal separation between the two feelings.[31]

---

[28] Ibid. 107.

[29] § 23, p. 91.

[30] Paul Guyer, 'Kant's Distinction Between the Beautiful and the Sublime', *Review of Metaphysics*, 35 (1982), 753–83. This reference p. 770.

[31] Ibid. 770.

There is good reason to reject both these explanations of Kant's vacillation. Neither of them explains why Kant likens the mental movement to a vibration (i.e. not just a succession of states, but a *repeated* succession thereof). Indeed, Guyer's second point is at odds with the fact that, both before and after Kant's use of the term 'judgement' (with its connotations of conscious concept application) in relation to the psychological process involved in the sublime, he consistently uses terms that strongly emphasize that we are not explicitly aware of this process. In this respect we are told that imagination '*betrays* its limits and inadequacy'[32] and that the '*inner perception*' of this inadequacy 'makes us alive to the feeling of the supersensible'—'whose pre-eminence can only be made *intuitively* evident' (my emphases added).[33] If Kant had even half-heartedly entertained the possibility that our awareness of the superiority of our rational faculty involved the mediation of conscious reflection rather than an indirect manifestation through feeling, he would have no grounds for his insistence that conventionally we mistakenly ascribe sublimity to the object which provokes it, instead of to our rational being. Given these considerations, a more plausible explanation of Kant's vacillation would be as follows. First (a point not noted by Guyer), in the two passages quoted earlier where Kant emphasizes the succession of feelings in the sublime, he is explicitly concerned with the contrast with our experience of 'restful contemplation' in beauty. Since a successive mental movement at levels of consciousness which are both explicit (in terms of feeling) and inexplicit (in terms of presenting ideas indeterminately) is the definitive feature of the sublime, he tends in the vibration analogy simply to over-emphasize it. Similar considerations hold (albeit from the opposite direction), in relation to Kant's claim about the 'simultaneous' experience of displeasure and pleasure in the sublime. For while we are dealing with a successive mental movement at two levels, Kant does need at some point to stress the phenomenological unity of this (i.e. that we experience it in terms of a *single* reflective judgement)—otherwise sublimity would not fit into the basic theoretical framework of the third *Critique*. On these terms, I would suggest that (overstatement

[32] *Judgement*, § 27, p. 106.
[33] Ibid. 107.

aside) Kant takes the experience of sublimity to involve a mental movement that is, temporally speaking, so rapid as to manifest itself at the explicitly conscious level only in a complex feeling where the elements of displeasure and pleasure cannot be discriminated as successive.

In § 27, then, Kant articulates both the moral significance and the phenomenology of judgements of mathematical sublimity. The importance of this former move becomes strikingly apparent in §§ 29 and 30, where Kant undertakes his Deduction of judgements of sublimity. His discussion centres on the notion of 'respect', which (as we have seen) is defined as 'The feeling of our capacity to attain to an idea that is a law for us'. I shall call this respect (2). We will also remember that, in the second *Critique*, Kant defines respect (hereafter referred to as 'respect (1)') as a feeling produced by our awareness that the moral law is binding upon us. This recognition that our will is necessarily subject to the moral law thwarts our sensuous inclinations and humiliates our self-conceit. In turn, this effect akin to pain clears away obstacles to morality and renews our sense of its superiority, and is thus the ground of a further positive feeling. Now clearly the analogy between respect (2) and (1) is not exact. The former is a process that involves an *inexplicit* awareness of the superiority of our rational being only at the second stage. The latter, in contrast, transpires entirely at the level of conscious awareness and involves knowledge of the superiority of our rational self (in the form of our recognition that the moral law is binding upon us) as both its premiss and, in an enhanced form, its conclusion. Nevertheless, there is still some element of affinity between the two in so far as both involve a mental movement from a state of negative to positive feeling, and the ultimate ground, indeed, of this positive feeling is the superiority of reason over sensibility.

The reason why Kant is so anxious to characterize the feeling of the sublime in terms of respect is that sublimity's putative moral aspect is made ultimately to sustain the burden of Kant's deduction of the necessity of judgements of sublimity. In relation to this topic, § 30 is instructively titled:

The deduction of aesthetic judgements upon objects of nature must not be directed to what we call sublime in nature, but only to the beautiful.[34]

---

[34] Ibid. § 30, p. 133.

Kant's reasoning here is based on the fact that beauty is constituted by a relation between the cognitive faculties achieved through the form of objects. Hence, if the pleasure we take in it is to claim universal validity it must be shown that we are justified in assuming a likeness of faculties amongst all subjects. With the sublime, in contrast, we are dealing with something which is not *constituted* by a relation between nature and our faculties, but should rather

in strictness, be attributed merely to the attitude of thought, or rather to that which serves as the basis for this in human nature. The apprehension of an object otherwise formless and in conflict with ends supplies the mere occasion for our coming to a consciousness of this basis.[35]

While Kant here asserts, in effect, that judgements of sublimity do not require a Deduction along the lines of those required by beauty, he is not naïve enough to suppose that no Deduction is required at all. Instead he takes himself to have already provided this in his preceding expository sections—and specifically through the link between sublimity and morality. In § 29 we are told that 'The proper mental mood for a feeling of the sublime postulates the mind's susceptibility for ideas.'[36]

Kant then links this susceptibility specifically to moral ideas, by claiming that, without the development and culture of moral ideas, that which we call sublime would simply strike us as terrifying. However, while the development of such ideas presupposes culture and society, such a capacity is not a mere product of social convention.

Rather it is in human nature that its foundations are laid, and, in fact, in that which, at once with common understanding, we may expect everyone to possess and may require of him, namely, a native capacity for the feeling for (practical) ideas, i.e. for moral feeling. [Hence] This, now, in the foundation of that agreement between other men's judgements on the sublime and our own, which we make our own imply.[37]

Kant holds, then, that to make judgements of sublimity presupposes a 'susceptibility' to moral feeling; and since we can assume such a susceptibility in all men, such judgements

---

[35] *Judgement*, § 27, p. 134.
[36] Ibid. § 29, p. 115.   [37] Ibid. 115.

can command universal assent. There are two fairly obvious objections to this view, both of which centre upon Kant's pivotal claim here that we can assume a universal susceptibility to moral feeling. The first of these consists in Kant's justification for this claim. Since there is little in the third *Critique* which would justify it, it is clear that Kant is here looking back to the position he takes himself to have established in the second *Critique*. There he asserts that, if we understand what the moral law is and what it demands, this will necessarily check our sensuous inclinations through the production—by an '*a priori* causality'—of the feeling of respect. But, as I argued in Chapter 2, Kant offers no compelling philosophical reason why we should accept this claim of moral feeling to a priori status. Indeed, even if we do allow it, it applies only to some notion of complex moral feeling as such. Kant is not entitled further to identify such feeling with that specific complex structure which he calls 'respect'. Hence, while on these terms a 'susceptibility' to complex moral feeling might be presupposed in all humans, this does not entail that its negative and positive aspects must likewise be articulated in just the same way in all human beings. In the case of judgements of sublimity this means that even if *we* experience the feeling of respect in response to some overwhelming natural item, we have no a priori entitlement to demand a similar response in others. They can be expected to have moral feeling but not necessarily our particular kind of moral susceptibility and insight. The natural item could simply strike *them* as overwhelming.

One must also express considerable unease over the very fact that Kant's deduction takes this exclusively moral form. While for him it is our supersensible aspect which is sublime, he by no means allows that the question of which natural items lead us to an awareness of this is an arbitrary one. Such items must both exceed our sensible grasp, and be able to evoke rational ideas. This means that another form of deduction is called for. As Paul Guyer succinctly puts it, 'The universal imputation of the judgement of sublimity presupposes that all persons have the same limits on their imagination, and that this Faculty will interact with reason in the same way in the case of any given object.'[38] Kant, however, offers no arguments to establish such

[38] *Kant and the Claims of Taste* (Harvard University Press: London and Cambridge, Mass., 1979), 265–6.

points. The moral aspect of the sublime unwarrantably eclipses all other considerations.

This completes my exposition of Kant's theory of the sublime. I shall now subject it to an overall critical review.

III

The general critical issues raised by Kant's theory of the sublime as a whole are enormous. For the purposes of this study (having already criticized his account of the epistemological status of judgements of sublimity), I shall concentrate on the theory's relationship to the remaining logical characteristics of the aesthetic judgement—namely disinterestedness (and the absence of definite concepts) on the one hand, and subjective finality on the other. In relation to the first of these, in Chapter 3, Section II, I showed that, for Kant, judgements of taste are aesthetic in character because our appreciation of an object's purely formal qualities is indifferent to the 'real existence' of the object. This means specifically that the grounds of our pleasure do not involve the desire that the object should really exist (in this respect an hallucination or mirage will do just as well as the real thing) and neither do they presuppose that we have a definite concept of what kind of thing the object is. It is clear that Kant regards judgements of the sublime as standing on a similar footing. In § 26, for example, we are told that

although we have no interest whatsoever in the Object, i.e. its real existence may be a matter of no concern to us, still its mere greatness regarded as even devoid of form, is able to convey a universally communicable delight, and so involve the consciousness of a subjective finality in the employment of our cognitive faculties.[39]

The question is how far this is really true of judgements of the sublime. Let us consider first the mathematical mode. In the initial stage of such judgements we imaginatively strive for, and feel frustrated at our failure to find, an absolute measure for some vast object. This (in Kant's terms) requires only the faculties of imagination and feeling as such. What kind of thing the object is, or our consciousness of it as real or illusory, have no bearing upon

[39] *Judgement*, § 25, p. 96.

this imaginative striving and the feeling consequent upon it. Here at least, therefore, is the *basis* of an argument for regarding this stage of judgements of the mathematically sublime as disinterested. Yet in relation to the second stage of such judgements, matters are entirely different. Here we take a pleasure in the fact that reason has demonstrated its superiority over sensibility. Given that for Kant our supersensible rational being is not only the true 'object' of sublimity but is our 'ultimate vocation', it follows that we must know this superiority to be real rather than illusory. Indeed, if such a superiority was experienced as anything less than real, it would hardly make the feeling of sublimity subjectively final in relation to moral feeling. It might even have the opposite effect—for if we were indifferent to the reality of theoretical reason's superiority over sensibility, this could incline us to be equally indifferent to morality's authority over our sensible being. Matters are also problematic in relation to Kant's holding that judgements of sublimity do not presuppose any definite concept of the object. He attempts to avoid any difficulty here by claiming that such judgements only present rational ideas (specifically those of infinity and the supersensible) 'indeterminately'. But consider Kant's following characterization of the rational idea in Remark 1 of § 57:

'A *rational idea* can never become a cognition, because it involves a concept (of the supersensible), for which a commensurate intuition can never be given.'[40]

Given this remark, a rational idea might be presented indeterminately in two ways—either because (by definition) it cannot be adequately schematized, or because it passes through our mind so quickly and confusedly as to elude explicit awareness. However, even if a rational idea is presented in these *psychologically* indeterminate ways, it still (in the terms of Kant's definition) *logically* presupposes the mediation of a 'concept (of the supersensible)'. One might bring out the full force of this point by way of a contrast. Whereas (as we saw in Chapter 3, Part II, of this study) our ability to enjoy judgements of taste does not presuppose the mastery of any specific concept (but involves, rather, the faculties of cognition as such), the judgement of mathematical sublimity, in contrast, presupposes that at some

[40] Ibid. § 57, p. 210.

stage in our life we have not only mastered the concepts of infinity and the supersensible, but also those which are required in order to become aware (however vaguely) of the superiority of our rational being over that of our sensible existence.

Some similar difficulties and a couple more besides accrue to Kant's theory of the dynamic sublime. First, we will remember that in judgements of this sort a state of imagined fear leads us to recognize that some natural object is mighty enough to render all physical resistance to it futile, but then leads us to imagine ourselves defying it through moral resolve. Now (leaving aside the question of what form such resolve would actually take) we will remember that Kant himself is at pains to stress, in § 28, that our imaginings here are not insincere or wishful thinking, but are countenanced as genuine possibilities of action. Here, far from being indifferent to the real existence of what we imagine, Kant holds that in the very roots of our rational being we desire its realization—even though we are not in circumstances where it could be so realized. There are also problems in relation to the role played by concepts in such judgements. In relation to their first stage, Kant talks as though there are two ways of appraising an object as mighty—either aesthetically by actual or imagined fear, or objectively via a concept. In the case of human beings, while some states of fear may reinforce our awareness that the object is mighty, such a state or imagined state would not arise in the first place unless we had some *reason* to be fearful (i.e. had judged that the object was powerful enough to destroy us). The mediation of the specific concept 'thing powerful enough to destroy me' is, in other words, logically presupposed—even if, psychologically speaking, one is not explicitly aware of it. Similar considerations hold in relation to the second stage, in so far as not only is the determinate concept of moral resolve or superiority involved, but also a determinate sensible element (i.e. a representation(s) embodying some morally edifying situation). Yet it may be that what Kant has in mind here is the notion of an aesthetic idea—an intuition of sense to which no determinate concept is adequate.[41] Might not this at least allow us to ascribe aesthetic significance to the second stage of the dynamic sublime? Unfortunately this serves only to highlight the problematic status

---

[41] See e.g. ibid. § 49, pp. 175–6.

of the aesthetic idea itself in Kant's overall theory. For while no specific concept may be adequate to an aesthetic idea, some such concept as 'moral superiority to nature' must mediate the play of imagination, if it is to be anything more than a mere train of random associations.

The second major area of overall difficulty which I shall consider in relation to Kant's theory of the sublime concerns the notion of 'subjective finality'. As we have seen, what gives judgements of taste this characteristic is the fact that our pleasure in them arises from a harmony of the faculties which is conducive to cognition generally. However, in the case of judgements of sublimity Kant's major pattern of argument construes them as subjectively final in a somewhat different sense (i.e. in relation to the 'higher ends of reason'). Kant's justification for this view depends (as we have seen) on the overall technical framework of the third *Critique*. If the realization of moral ends (i.e. our supersensible 'vocation') is the final end of all creation, then imagination's inadequacy in relation to the scope of our rational supersensible being (while contra-final in relation to cognition) is nevertheless in full accordance or harmony with this final *moral* end. Indeed, in so far as in such judgements our sensible being is humiliated by our supersensible dimension, the feeling founded on this relation is itself of indirect moral significance. It is a mode of 'respect'. Although this broader context does show how imagination and reason can be said to be in harmony through their conflict, it cannot, nevertheless, be the whole story. For all that the above approach establishes is that judgements of sublimity are of *indirect moral significance*. They involve nature and subjective finality—but these facts do not seem to contribute anything positive to the experience. We simply have something which shows the triumph of reason over imagination, in a way that roughly parallels the moral law's humiliation of our sensible being in the feeling of respect. This is the most fundamental problem with Kant's theory of the sublime as a whole. The fact that here it is a feeling rather than a concept which is final in relation to morality is, for Kant, sufficient to establish that judgements of sublimity are 'subjectively determined' and thence aesthetic in character. But from a general critical viewpoint this is most unsatisfactory. If the aesthetic is to be a distinctive mode of feeling, our criteria of it must be *logical*, that is, we must establish that the grounds or factors which occasion it are unique, rather than explicable in terms of those which occasion other types of feeling. In the case of sublimity, however, Kant fails to do this. His criteria of such judgements are *psychological* inasmuch as they hinge on 'indeterminate' lessons of moral significance which we learn from our cognitive engagement with nature.

A more promising approach would have been to argue that the subjective finality involved in judgements of sublimity to some degree parallels that involved in judgements of taste: that our experience of the former involves not just a humiliation of imagination by reason but an additional more harmonious element. Fortunately, at a number of scattered points in the Analytic of the Sublime, Kant does indeed offer the basis of just such an argument. For example, in § 25, we are told that our pleasure in the sublime is 'a delight in an extension affecting the imagination itself'.[42] Again, in § 29, Kant declares that in judgements of the sublime, reason engages sensibility 'with a view to extending it to the requirements of its own realm . . . and letting it look out beyond itself into the infinite, which for it [i.e. sensibility] is an abyss'.[43]

On these terms, in judgements of sublimity imagination does not just function negatively as a dimension of pain; it also enjoys an exhilarating sense of being extended beyond its limits. The demands of reason lead it to grapple with the formless object, and, under the influence of the rational idea which the struggle gives rise to, imagination's initial pain is thereby transformed into a 'feeling of unboundedness'. Given the fact that here the imagination is construed as having a positive as well as a negative role, we have, in effect, a feature which separates judgements of sublimity from that feeling of the sublime (i.e. 'respect') which arises from exclusively moral contexts. We have a felt harmony of the faculties in which sensibility (to some degree) gains from its inadequacy to meet the demands of reason—in a way that it does not, in the context of moral judgements. This is why the ambiguity noted in Section II of this chapter (in relation to Kant's analysis of the phenomenological structure of the feeling of the sublime) proves ultimately so telling. If Kant wants to

---

[42] *Judgement*, § 25, p. 96. See also § 26, p. 100, and § 29, p. 127.
[43] Ibid. § 29, p. 115.

establish the aesthetic credentials of sublimity he must not present it as a simple transition from pleasure to pain. This would place it too close to moral respect. Instead he must show it to be a complex feeling of attraction and repulsion, thus bringing out the fact that imagination's role is more than merely negative. Indeed, it may be that this need to stress imagination's active dimension is responsible for that emphasis on searching out infinity as an absolute measure which (as I showed in Section II of Chapter 4) Kant uses to explain the mathematical sublime. If Kant had stressed this positive dimension of imagination unambiguously his overall position would have been greatly strengthened. On the one hand he could have offered (without concealing their differences) an argument for what gives judgements of beauty and sublimity their common aesthetic character, and on the other hand he could have differentiated the sublimity of our moral being from the aesthetic experience of it. That Kant does not do this is due to the pressures exerted by his Critical ethics. In Chapter 2 I showed that Kant had there, in effect, arrived at the position that only our supersensible moral being is worthy of the term 'sublime'. This would explain his eagerness in the third *Critique* to disallow natural objects from being so described. However, the above account of how he ought to have presented judgements of sublimity would not have impinged on these considerations. It may be that our moral being alone is worthy of the term sublime, but it is, nevertheless, only formless objects which can make us aware of this moral sublimity in a way that has positive consequences for sensibility. This (as Kant himself hints in § 25[44]) would actually reinforce our sense of the sublimity of our moral being, in so far as we here find its traces even in our aesthetic judgements of formless nature. One would, therefore, with every justification call such objects aesthetically sublime, in order to pick out this privileged role.

I have, then, elaborated and criticized the development and structure of Kant's theory of the sublime. In his Critical ethics it is conceived in moral terms and then transposed into an aesthetic concept in the third *Critique*. I argued that, in that work, Kant's fundamental organizational principles are directed

---

[44] I am here referring specifically to Kant's passing remark that 'it is the use to which judgement . . . puts particular objects on behalf of [moral feeling] . . . that is absolutely great' (ibid. § 25, p. 97).

towards showing—however clumsily—that if morality is the final end of all creation, then there must be something about both the way we order nature (in theoretical terms) and our status as sensible creatures of feeling that is indirectly conducive to morality. The a priori principle of natural finality provides the point of connection here. This is because, on the one hand, it leads us to think of nature as a hierarchy of ends with morality as the ultimate one; and on the other hand—through subjective finality—it is the determining ground of our pleasure in aesthetic judgements. Kant presumes in this latter case that, because our feeling is here determined by an a priori (and thence supersensible) principle, this will make it all the easier for morality to determine our sensibility. Indeed, while the grounds of judgements of taste are logically independent of those of morality, it is their conduciveness to morality which is at the heart of their claims to universality, and which forms, metaphysically speaking, their *raison d'être*. Given this approach to judgements of taste, sublimity takes on an important role in the underlying strategy of the third *Critique*. Kant can only broach the links between taste and morality in the most circumspect way. This is because, as he explains them, judgements of taste are sufficiently accounted for in terms of the harmony of imagination and understanding. To introduce an additional moral dimension too soon and too explicitly might be seen as casting doubt on the credibility of his main explanation. In the case of judgements of sublimity, in contrast, there is actually room for such a broader perspective. For the influential precedent of Burke already suggests that sublimity is a psycho-logically complex experience of pain and pleasure, involving factors pertaining to an awareness of our finitude. Hence, it is only to be expected that, while being in some sense an aesthetic judgement, sublimity will also connect up with broader aspects of human experience. Burke's precedent therefore provides a context in relation to which the close links which Kant makes between morality and sublimity would not, in themselves, immediately challenge the latter's claim to aesthetic status. Kant's theory of the sublime, in other words, fits in rather better with the underlying strategy of the third *Critique* as a whole than does his theory of beauty. However, as we have seen, this architectonic success is bought at a price. For Kant is so keen to stress the moral aspects of sublimity that he fails to offer anything convincing—apart from scattered hints—as to its credentials as an aesthetic concept. Indeed, in the Deduction he takes a short cut whereby the judgement of sublimity's claim to universality is construed as a function of the unwarranted assumption of a susceptibility to moral feeling in all humans. In the final analysis, the pressures exerted by his Critical ethics prove too great. Our experience of sublimity in relation to nature is reduced to indirect moral awareness.

Given the difficulties I have raised, the question arises as to whether Kant's theory can still be made generally viable. I would suggest that it can. To effect this task will involve the abandonment of Kant's overall architechtonics (including the doctrine of the faculties), his main 'baroque' version of the mathematical sublime, and his *entire treatment of the dynamical mode, and the Deduction*. The basis of my alternative theory will involve the retention of the 'mathematical' and 'dynamic' as categories—but restated on the common basis of both a revision of Kant's minor 'austere' approach to the mathematical sublime, and his scattered insights concerning sensibility having a positive role in the experience. Armed with this revised theory I will then consider the deferred question of why Kant excludes artworks from judgements of sublimity, and will offer arguments to show that such artefacts can, in fact, be encompassed by the sublime. I will then draw some broader conclusions.

It is to these tasks of revision and extension that I now turn, in the final chapters of this study.

PART III

Artifice, Metaphysics, and the Sublime

6

A Reconstruction of Kant's Theory of the Sublime

I

If Kant's theory of the sublime is to be reworked into a viable form and developed in the direction of its full potential, then this reconstructive task should be located within a more general theory of aesthetic judgements, of which the experience of the sublime will form one distinctive variety. To outline such a theory in the requisite detail would involve a major study in itself. However, by reworking Kant's account of the judgement of taste, we will at least have the plausible *basis* of some general criteria of the aesthetic, which can then be shown to encompass judgements of sublimity.

As a starting-point, we will remember that Kant characterizes pure aesthetic judgements in terms of their disinterestedness, universality, subjective finality, and necessity. For the purposes of reconstruction I will concentrate on the first and third of these—since they concern the *grounds* of our aesthetic responses, rather than their more general epistemological status. First, then, the notion of disinterestedness.

For Kant, our judgements of taste have this characteristic in so far as they are 'apart' from any definite concept, and are indifferent to the 'real existence' of the object. Kant's claims here can, I would suggest, be read independently of the overall Critical system in the following way. To appreciate the formal qualities of an object (i.e. the relationships of such features as line, mass, density, shape, and texture) is to appreciate the structural aspects of the way it is presented to the senses alone. Hence, our enjoyment of such qualities does not presuppose that we know anything about the object—not even such basic facts as what it is, what functions it serves, or whether or not it is anything more than a mere appearance. Of course, characteristically we will in fact know a great deal about the object, but the point is that such knowledge is not presupposed *in order* to enjoy the structure of its appearance. On these terms, we might logically characterize such aesthetic judgements as *absolutely disinterested* inasmuch as their exercise entails no necessary reference to that broader network of practical needs, knowledge, and interests which constitutes our normal everyday orientation to the world.

Given that our judgements of taste are absolutely disinterested, the question arises as to *why* we take a pleasure in the discrimination of such formal qualities. We should be able to ground the logical characteristic of disinterestedness on some plausible explanation of the *phenomenological* structure of aesthetic judgements. It is this task which Kant undertakes through relating such judgements to the notion of subjective finality (i.e. a harmonious interplay of imagination and under-standing which is conducive to our cognitive life in general). Again, I would suggest that something like Kant's point here can be expressed in terms independent of his overall Critical system. Let us begin from the indisputable fact that as rational beings human subjects have the capacity to conceptualize, that is, to make cognitive discriminations and classifications. This capacity is generally employed in a perceptually undeliberative manner, in so far as we simply *recognize* that such and such an object satisfies such and such a concept or description. However, there are occasions when our conceptualization of some object does involve a process of perceptual deliberation—as, for example, when we have difficulty in deciding what term applies to the item under consideration, or when we wish to discover how, or how well, its parts cohere in terms of the unity defined by the kind of thing it is. On occasion such perceptual deliberation is found pleasurable. We enjoy, say, the fact that we have discovered what kind of thing the unfamiliar object is, or what function it serves; or we enjoy the way it looks to be a perfect instance of its kind, or the anticipation of the efficient performance which it promises. In most such cases we will be able to explain our pleasure ultimately in terms of the object's relation to the broader network of our theoretical or practical aims and interests. If we recognize some puzzling object in terms of some familiar concept or theory it serves to confirm the continuing validity or utility of such notions. Our outlook on the world is felt as *secure* and thence satisfying. We may also experience pleasure simply on the grounds of our own cleverness in solving the problem. In relation to more ostensibly practical matters, similar considerations hold, inasmuch as here we may enjoy looking at the object because of some anticipation of how well it will fulfil its function. But if our pleasure in the object is absolutely disinterested, we will not be able to account for it in such terms. We must, therefore, ask why our perceptual deliberation upon formal qualities alone is found pleasurable? In Section II of Chapter 3 in this study, I suggested that when Kant asserts that the judgement of taste involves the faculties of cognition as such (rather than any specific concept) we can make sense of this in terms of the psychological complexity of such judgements. Given a rich and diverse sensory manifold we do not simply recognize it 'as' *an x*, rather we judge the many different relations which hold between part and part, and part and whole, in the manifold. Indeed, because our conceptualizing activity is so complex here, we are conscious, fundamentally, only of the pleasure it gives rise to. By adopting this interpretation of Kant's position we have an explanation of judgements of taste which need make no reference to the doctrine of the faculties. We would simply say that the judgement of taste invokes our capacity for cognitive discrimination in a way that is more complex and heightened than normal.

The fact that this heightened activity is a response to the diversity of a particular sensible manifold rather than to some problem or function related to the network of our theoretical and practical interests also provides a plausible basis for explaining the grounds of our aesthetic pleasure. To see why this is so, we must first make a few remarks about the distinction between our rational and sensible being which is so important to Kant's overall position. To account for this distinction in terms of the supersensible/phenomenal dichotomy is, I think, utterly implausible. However, it is clear that our rationality is something which (to whatever degree) sets us apart from the natural world. We *feel* that we can and do think and act in a way that cannot be reduced to the causal mechanisms which determine the natural order. It may be that our rational capacities can be explained purely as a function of our sensible embodiment; it may also be the case that some deterministic explanation of this function can be offered; but from the viewpoint of everyday existence, we at least proceed *as if* we have a rational capacity that is independent of natural causality. Given this, it remains, nevertheless, true that as embodied creatures of sensibility and feeling we are still a part of the natural world. Reason and our membership of a domain of sensible existents constitute the two fundamental aspects of the human condition. The question now arises, therefore, as to how these relate? In this respect, it is reasonable to suppose that the achievement of psychological states wherein the two aspects are embodied in some harmonious relation will yield a special sense of unity and security—of feeling 'at home' in the world. But states such as these are the exception rather than the rule. For the most part, reason functions as the 'slave' of sensibility. It seeks out the means to realize ends bound up with the needs of our physiological, material, and emotional existence as sensible beings. More exceptionally this capacity is employed for its own sake—especially in those contexts where we seek theoretical knowledge purged of undue influence from interests bound up with our immediate practical and sensible existence. Now I would suggest that, in contrast to the one-sided relation which holds in these cases of the interplay of rational cognition and interests connected with our membership of the sensible world, the aesthetic judgement embodies them in a more harmonious relationship. In this respect, the following remark from Schiller proves instructive.

In order to lay hold of the fleeting phenomenon . . . [the philosopher] must first bind it in fetters of rule, tear its fair body to pieces by reducing it to concepts, and preserve its living spirit in a sorry skeleton of words.[1]

Though Schiller's remark here has a specific application, it is surely an apt—if dramatic—evocation of our rational capacity in its general cognitive employment. For to form and apply concepts is to abstract from—and in a sense denude—that sensible world of which we are a part. In the aesthetic judgement, however, we exercise our capacity for cognitive discrimination in a way that is in harmony with the particular sensible manifold. We are led perceptually to deliberate upon it for its own

[1] F. Schiller, *Letters on the Aesthetic Education of Mankind*, ed. E. Wilkinson and L. Willoughby (Clarendon Press: Oxford, 1982), 5.

sake. Indeed, the richer the sensible manifold, the more heightened and deliberative our cognitive activity becomes. We find ourselves undergoing an experience wherein a rational capacity and the sensible world are mutually enhancing, but where there are none of the psychological pressures usually associated with the demands and interests of everyday life. One might say that we enjoy aesthetic judgements because they embody a *felt compatibility* between rational cognition and the sensible realm. In such experience, we are truly 'at home' in the world.

I have argued that Kant's notions of disinterestedness and the harmony of understanding and imagination can be restated in a rather modified form, so as to provide plausible logical and phenomenological criteria of the aesthetic judgement. But the question arises as to why we should take these criteria to be definitive of the aesthetic as such. It is clear that our deepest appreciation of art could hardly count as absolutely disinterested, since its 'real existence' is a matter of profound concern to us. We desire that the art object be real rather than a forgery or hallucination. It has also been argued by R. W. Hepburn that Kantian criteria are even inadequate in relation to a number of putatively aesthetic aspects of our experience of nature. Suppose we take pleasure in the sturdiness of an oak tree, only to find that it is rotten to the core. Would not the discovery of this fact about the 'real existence' of the tree totally spoil our pleasure? Again, suppose we are standing in the midst of a desolate moor. Here, Hepburn suggests, we might experience the following:

'I had seen from the map that this was a deserted moor, but not till I stood in the middle of it did I realize its desolation.' Here 'realize' involves making or becoming, vivid to perception, or to the imagination.[2]

This means that aesthetic 'realization' is subject to truth, in that the discovery that other people were on the moor would spoil our pleasure in its desolation. This brings us to the fundamental point of contention. Does the fact that such pleasure can be affected by the truth of the appraisal on which it is founded disqualify it—as the out and out Kantian formalist would hold—

[2] R. W. Hepburn, *Wonder: And Other Essays* (Edinburgh University Press: Edinburgh, 1984) 27.

from aesthetic status, or is this merely a different variety of aesthetic experience? Hepburn asserts the latter view. For, given the formalist's interest in unity and diversity and the like,

One could argue that reference to truth—the striving to 'realize'—should be taken as adding one more level of complexity, a further challenge to our power of synopsis, and that for the exclusion of it no good reason could be given.[3]

Yet against this, one might retort that if such 'realizations' are to warrant the term 'aesthetic' Hepburn must show what it is that they have in common with what is more generally regarded as aesthetic experience, namely the appreciation of strictly formal qualities. Hepburn does not offer such an argument. But we can provide the basis of one by slightly modifying Kant's criteria of the aesthetic.

In this respect, let us first be clear about the contrast between realizations and judgements of taste. The grounds of the former mode of appreciation are, logically speaking, restricted. They presuppose knowledge of both a specific concept and its relation to a specific state of affairs, in a way that the absolutely disinterested appreciation of purely formal qualities does not. The crucial point is, however, that such realizations can at least be characterized as *relatively disinterested*. This is because we can enjoy the sturdiness of the oak or the desolation of the moor for their own sake, rather than for the relevance of such qualities to the broader network of our practical or purely theoretical aims and interests. Indeed, Hepburn's phenomenological characterization of these realizations goes some way towards explaining why we take a pleasure in them. For to realize the 'sturdiness' of the oak or the 'desolation' of the moor is to make those qualities 'vivid' to perception or imagination. This means that we do not simply recognize the oak tree or the moor as characterizable in terms of the concepts 'sturdiness' and 'desolation' (respectively); instead our sense of what these abstract general terms mean or involve is heightened and clarified by deliberation upon the very richness of nature's sensuous particularity. In the case of our appreciation of strictly formal qualities, I argued that our pleasure was grounded in a felt compatibility between rational cognition and the sensible world. This, I would suggest,

---

[3] R. W. Hepburn, *Wonder: And Other Essays*, 27.

is also the case with realizations. Here we enjoy the felt compatibility between a particular exercise of rational cognition and the sensible domain, rather than the more general sense of compatibility which characterizes the judgement of taste. One must of course say that the latter is, logically speaking, the 'purest' form of aesthetic experience, but this does not imply that its quality of felt compatibility is in any sense superior to that involved in realizations; one supposes that such experiences will simply tend to *feel different* from one another. The former, for example, might most often be characterized by a kind of leisurely perceptual exploration of the manifold, while the latter might most frequently take the form of a sudden pleasing sense of surprise.

These considerations lead to several important conclusions. First, they show that the Kantian criteria whereby we plausibly characterized the judgement of taste have modified application in a broader context. This suggests that we should regard the aesthetic not as a single mode of experience, but as a domain of logically and phenomenologically cognate experiences at once definable and differentiable in terms of the contrasting senses of disinterestedness they involve, and in terms of their contrasting ways of embodying the felt compatibility of rational cognition with the sensible world. The general strength of this approach is that it allows us to escape from the unwarrantably restrictive definitions of the aesthetic propounded by traditional formalism, yet without succumbing to scepticism as to the very possibility of finding criteria for the aesthetic. The implications of this approach are equally fruitful for the specific purposes of this study. So far, I have illustrated something of the breadth of the aesthetic domain through the example of judgements of taste and realizations alone. Elsewhere,[4] however, I have shown how the notions of perfection, and art, might likewise be encompassed by this approach. It also has other possibilities, one of which—at last—is its application to our experience of the sublime. I shall, therefore, now offer my revision of Kant's theory of the sublime, with a view to locating it securely within the aesthetic domain in general.

---

[4] See e.g. my paper 'The Claims of Perfection: A Revisionary Defence of Kant's Theory of Dependent Beauty', *International Philosophical Quarterly*, 26:1 (Mar. 1986), 61–74.

II

I shall first address the mathematical sublime, that is, that mode which is embodied in our encounter with *vast* objects. It will be recalled that, in § 26 of the third *Critique*, Kant distinguishes between the mathematical and the aesthetic estimation of magnitude. The former involves judging the size of an object by calculating (according to a numerical rule) how many times an object will fit into some given unit of measure. The latter is done 'in intuition, by the eye alone'. The real basis of Kant's distinction here is not a contrast between a mode of judgement that involves a concept and a mode of judgement that does not, but between formal and informal conceptualisations of size. Clearly, mathematical estimates are highly formalized, but what sort of informality is it that could lead Kant to talk of 'aesthetic' estimates? One might answer as follows. A child learns such things as size and distances by physical exploration of its environment. It conceptualizes as 'big' those objects which it finds hard to cope with in tems of the exercise of its physical capacities. The articulation of such 'bigness' in terms of determinate mathematical concepts is something which is subsequently built on these foundations. Given this, we might say that the child's initial conceptualization is 'aesthetic' (i.e. subjectively determined), not because it lacks a rule of judgement, but because that rule is derived and applied informally, on the basis of reference to the child's physical frame and capacities.

Now this 'aesthetic' mode of estimating size is something which never leaves us. An adult can gauge the size of a mountain through applying mathematical rules (e.g. 'it's about two or three thousand feet high') or alternatively by such things as imagining that it would take a great deal of effort to climb, or by noting how insignificant a speck the person at present climbing the mountain seems to be. In practice, most of our estimations of size are of this latter sort, in so far as the needs and interests which orientate us towards the world rarely demand mathematical exactitude. However, let us suppose that we wish not only to estimate the size of the mountain, but to grasp it in its phenomenal totality—to form an image that fully expresses just how big the object is, in relation to our physical frame and capacities. Here the attempt to form an aesthetic estimate becomes acutely problematic. Even if we were to explore every part of the mountain by foot (or by telescope) our imagination would soon be overwhelmed by the plethora of parts. As Kant puts it:

if the apprehension has reached a point beyond which the representations of sensuous intuition in the case of the parts first apprehended begin to disappear from the imagination as this advances to the apprehension of yet others, as much, then, is lost at one end as is gained at the other, and for comprehension we get a maximum which the imagination cannot exceed.[5]

Yet if we are confronted by a vast object whose phenomenal totality in relation to the human frame cannot be grasped in perceptual or imaginative terms, we can and do, nevertheless, conceptualize it as a totality in purely *rational* terms.—Indeed there is no limit to such rational comprehension inasmuch as we can conceive infinity itself, and the insignificance of our relation to it. This means that the very fact that the scope of our conceptualizing capacity ranges beyond the limitations of our sensible finite nature is made vivid by the vast object itself. To put it in Hepburn's terms, the sensible object 'realizes' the scope of rational conceptualization precisely (and paradoxically) because it cannot be grasped as a totality at the perceptual and imaginative level. It is this 'realization', I would suggest, that accounts for our pleasure in the mathematical sublime. In such an experience, we feel ourselves as transcending the limits imposed by embodiment.

Having offered a reconstructed version of Kant's notion of the mathematical sublime, I shall now adopt a similar strategy in relation to the dynamical mode (but without making any use of Kant's arguments specifically concerned with it). First, one might parallel Kant's distinction between mathematical and aesthetic estimates of magnitude with one between mathematical and aesthetic estimates of *power*. For example, using such units of measure as miles per hour, or horsepower, one can express the power exerted by natural phenomena or artefacts in essentially mathematical terms. The child, however, initially learns to conceptualize degrees of power by the capacity of objects,

---

[5] Kant, *Judgement*, § 26, p. 99.

persons, and (indeed) institutions to inflict physical harm or restriction upon his body, possessions, and environment. Again, this mode of estimation is the one which carries over most extensively into adult life. One can measure the power of earthquakes on the Richter scale, but, unless one is a geophysicist, it is much more customary to estimate it in terms of the fatalities, injuries, and damage it causes. But why is it that destructive power and its effects on the natural and human world should be a source of pleasure to us? Burke's strategy (as shown in Chapter 1) is to suggest that, through being experienced from a position of safety, the terror that we would normally experience in the face of might is tinged with delight. Yet this would not only fail to distinguish the feeling of the sublime from mere relief, but would also fail to differentiate it from those cases where we feel genuine terror, even though the fearful object is a safe distance away. Kant, in contrast, suggests that, although we recognize that some object has the capacity to destroy us, we can, from a position of safety, imagine ourselves as morally resistant even in the face of destruction. I have rehearsed the objections to this view at length in preceding chapters, and these are, I think, so serious as to rule out a reconstruction on exactly these moral lines. To explain our pleasure in the dynamical sublime, therefore, it is more fruitful once more to invoke Hepburn's notion of realization. One might proceed as follows. As noted above, we can estimate the power of a destructive object by reference to the havoc it wreaks. However, if we are dealing with an object of extreme destructive power, we may have to consider possible or actual effects so enormously devastating as to exceed our perceptual and imaginative capacities. For example, suppose we witness an avalanche in the distance. We know that it could destroy us and others many many times over, and cause great devastation to the environment. If we try to imagine the totality of fear, suffering, and devastation that the avalanche is, or might be, causing, a limit is soon reached. Indeed, even if we survey the aftermath, the totality of devastation may be too much to comprehend in perceptual terms. But from a rational viewpoint, not only can we comprehend the power of the avalanche and the havoc it wreaks, we can even conceptualize the idea of infinite power and the insignificance of our relation to it. The mighty object, in other words, 'realizes' the fact that our conceptualizing capacity can even range over power that, from the perceptual and imaginative viewpoint of a finite creature, is incomprehensible as a totality. This, I would suggest, explains our pleasure in the dynamical sublime.

Let me now place this reconstructed version of Kant's theory of the sublime in a broader context. First, suppose that while in the desert we experience the mirage of a vast mountain range and that this encounter is experienced in terms of a feeling of sublimity. Suppose also that we then become aware that the mountain range *is*, in fact, a mirage. Would this discovery have any bearing on the grounds of our pleasure? In the strictest terms, it ought not to. For the scope of rational cognition can be 'realized' just as much by the *appearance* of vastness and power, as it can by the vastness or power of a real object. That this is so is amply evidenced (as I will show in the next chapter) by the fact that we can experience sublimity through representations of vast or powerful objects in works of art. It follows, therefore, that we can characterize judgements of sublimity as disinterested in so far as they do not presuppose any knowledge as to whether the object is real or illusory. This sense of disinterestedness together with that arising from the fact that our pleasure here does not presuppose reference to a background context of practical or theoretical interests serves to give sublimity a close logical kinship to the judgement of taste. Indeed, one might say that, just as the judgement of taste involves (as it were) a felt *qualitative* compatibility between cognition and the diverse particularity of the sensible world, the judgement of sublimity embodies a felt *quantitative* compatibility. No matter how vast or mighty the phenomenal object we can always conceptualize the totality of such vastness and power. Despite this, however, judgements of sublimity are relatively rather than absolutely disinterested in so far as they presuppose a quite specific element which judgements of taste do not. To appreciate the formal qualities of an object, for example, requires that we can discriminate between the parts in a sensible manifold, but it does not require that we know what kind of thing the object is. In the judgement of sublimity, in contrast, while it is not presupposed that we know whether the object is real or not, it is presupposed that we can at least recognize it *as* an 'overwhelmingly vast' or 'overwhelmingly powerful' manifold; that is, one whose parts we can discriminate, but could never hope to comprehend as a totality in perceptual or imaginative terms.

It is crucial to note that this presupposition is fundamentally a logical one. For we do not need to posit the necessary mediation of an *occurrent* psychological state of displeasure or felt privation at our sensible limitations on every occasion that we experience the sublime. It may be that, when faced with the vast or mighty object, we do *sometimes* (indeed, perhaps often—in ways described earlier) engage in a fruitless and thence frustrating struggle to comprehend its totality in perceptual or imaginative terms. But the point is that we do not have to. The background knowledge of our sensible limitations (ingrained in us from childhood) can enable us simply to *recognize* the object as overwhelming, without involving us in any 'painful' perceptual struggle with it. This means that in order for the scope of rational comprehension to be made vivid by a vast or mighty object, all that is presupposed is a knowledge of our sensible limitations in relation to that object. One of the reasons why Kant, Burke, and others have placed such emphasis on the supposedly necessary mediation of an occurrent state of privation or displeasure is to explain why, psychologically speaking, the feeling of sublimity is characteristically one of awe, or astonishment, or exhilaration, etc., rather than the restful contemplation we enjoy in relation to beauty. The explanation I have offered does cope adequately with this point. For while it is an aspect of the sensible world which makes the scope of rational cognition vivid to the senses and thus embodies a feeling of compatibility, it is, nevertheless, a background knowledge of the particular limitations of human sensibility which makes this broader feeling of compatibility possible. The sublime is thus, at heart, both a paradoxical and intense experience. It is the sensible world in its excess which limits perceptual cognition, yet it is a particular instance of this excess which gives the scope of rational cognition such a dramatic impact. We feel ourselves to be both imprisoned and liberated by the very same force. This, I would suggest, is why the felt compatibility between world and cognition in the experience of sublimity takes the form of awe and astonishment, or even ecstatic bewilderment.

I have argued that the sublime is one distinctive form of experience within an aesthetic domain definable by various senses of disinterestedness and felt compatibility between cognition and the sensible world. One might say that sublimity is to be located somewhere between the judgement of taste and those rather narrower cases of realization noted earlier. In offering this theory, I have considerably reconstructed Kant's approach in the third *Critique*. However, most of the basic insights which I have built upon are fundamentally his. It now only remains for me to turn to the long deferred discussion of the relation between sublimity and art.

7

Sublimity, Art, and Beyond

I

Having reconstructed Kant's theory of the sublime in general aesthetic terms, I shall now consider in what sense, direct or modified, it applies in the particular case of art. It is interesting in this respect that, while Kant himself does not rule out a link between sublimity and art, he treats it as of secondary importance, in so far as judgements in such a context would involve teleological considerations and would thereby lack 'pure' aesthetic status. Kant's illustration of this point in § 26 is as follows—

we must not point to the sublime in works of art, e.g. buildings, statues and the like, where a human end determines the form as well as the magnitude, nor yet in things of nature, *that in their very concept import a definite end* e.g. animals of a recognised natural order, but in rude nature merely as involving magnitude.[1]

However, in going on to say why natural objects with a definite end cannot be sublime, Kant makes a move which shows precisely why, in some circumstances, such objects *can* be sublime—

For in a representation of this kind nature contains nothing monstrous (nor what is either magnificent or horrible)—the magnitude may be increased to any extent provided imagination is able to grasp it all in one whole. An object is *monstrous* where by its size it defeats the end that forms its concept.[2]

Kant thus gives the circumstances in which, say, an animal of a definite species could be sublime. It would have to be of so monstrous a size that, psychologically speaking, we are so engrossed in the act of trying perceptually to apprehend its enormity that we pay no attention to (indeed are wholly

---

[1] *Judgement*, § 26, p. 100.   [2] Ibid. 100.

distracted from) the kind of animal it is. In this case the animal's very size is 'contra-final'.

Given that a natural object can be sublime despite having a definite end, surely this can also apply to works of artifice—if they are big enough? Kant himself shows the viability of this claim, by inconsistently using works of architecture to illustrate the phenomenological workings of the sublime generally—and not simply of some putatively 'impure' mode. For example, when a visitor first arrives at St Peter's in Rome,

a feeling comes home to him of the inadequacy of his imagination for presenting the idea of a whole within which that imagination attains its maximum, and, in its fruitless efforts to extend this limit, recoils upon itself, but in so doing succumbs to an emotional delight.[3]

On these terms (to put Kant's point in terms of my reconstruction of his theory), a work of artifice can be so perceptually overwhelming as to transcend our sense of its human origin, and serve simply to make vivid the scope of our capacity for rational cognition. However, Kant's example can also be made to reveal another possibility. Suppose that the visitor to St Peter's studies its architecture and the history of its construction, and those who designed and built it. If he should still feel astonishment, we would perhaps be reluctant to construe the grounds of his response on exactly the lines noted above, because he has been so *profoundly* imbued with an inescapable sense of its artifice. I would suggest that, in a case such as this, the sense of one's perception being overwhelmed and unable to comprehend the basilica's full phenomenal magnitude remains. What has changed, though, is the human capacity which is made vivid. Instead of the scope of rational cognition as such, it is, rather, a sense of the scope of human artifice which is thrown into relief. One can glean from a book that such and such a building, or dam, or monument, or whatever, is an impressive feat of engineering, but it is only in the perceptually overwhelming presence of the object itself that we feel an authentic astonishment at what human creativity can achieve. This harmonious tension between what is perceptually overwhelming and what is nevertheless known to be artifice provides, I would suggest, the basis

---

[3] Ibid. 100.

for one aspect of a specifically artistic sense of the sublime (construing 'artistic' here in the broadest possible sense).

I shall develop this notion more fully further on in this chapter. Before that I will consider a second difficulty which Kant raises in respect of the purity of judgements of sublimity in relation to art. In § 23 of the third *Critique* we are told that such judgements 'are always restricted by the conditions of an agreement with nature'.[4] Kant's meaning here is left obscure and unelaborated, but he is, I think, applying the point noted earlier (concerning the difficulty of enjoying sublimity in relation to objects with a definite end) to the particular case of representational art. For if the function of such works is to represent the world, the way in which their signifying elements are ordered must in a sense be in 'agreement with nature'; that is, we must be able to read the poem or painting (or whatever) as referring to that specific or imaginary state (or states) of affairs in the world which forms its subject-matter or content. However, the question which must be asked is whether (as I take him to imply) this required correspondence between a representation and a subject-matter must *necessarily* count as a restriction on our experiencing such a work as sublime? In a well-known footnote late on in Book I of the third *Critique*, Kant moves in a direction that is rather at odds with his implied position in the main body of the text. We are told that

Perhaps there has never been a more sublime utterance, or a thought more sublimely expressed, than the well known inscription upon the Temple of *Isis* (Mother *Nature*): 'I am all that is, and that was, and that ever shall be, and no mortal hath raised the veil from my face'.[5]

These remarks present several lines of approach. First, Kant now clearly concedes that representational artworks *can* have a content or subject-matter which *in itself* is in some sense sublime. As in the case of the inscription upon the Temple of Isis, we may be dealing with ideas whose intellectual content cannot be totally grasped in any perceptual or imaginative sense, or which evoke extremes of terror and fantasy. Similar considerations can hold in relation to the visual arts. Bernini's *Vision of St Theresa* deals with a momentary encounter between the infinite (and therefore perceptually and imaginatively incomprehensible) Godhead, and

---

[4] *Judgement*, § 23, p. 91.   [5] Ibid. § 49, pp. 178–9.

a finite being. More familiar still, there is a whole genre of 'sublime' landscape painting produced between about 1750 and 1850—towering mountain ranges, raging storms, bottomless crevasses, blasted heaths, threatened travellers, etc., etc. Now, given that art can have such subject-matter, there is no intrinsic reason why, if one is sensitive (or, less charitably, fanciful) enough, one should not be totally carried away by the artist's vision. One senses that—were it to be encountered in reality— one could never hope perceptually to grasp *this* (depicted) mountain range, but one could nevertheless conceptualize its vastness. It is likely that, during the originary epoch of the Gothic novel and sublime landscape, the artistic audience was indeed 'transported', that is, responded to the represented subject-matter in much the same terms as they would respond to the experience of it in real life. Unfortunately, once the treatment of a sublime subject-matter consolidated into a conventional genre, it became much more difficult to respond in such terms. This is probably one of the reasons why the sublime has become generally debased as an aesthetic concept. The infinite vistas and terrifying events become mere signifiers of an outmoded theatricality.

However, it will be remembered that in reference to the inscription on the Temple of Isis Kant uses the term 'sublime' not only in relation to the 'utterance' itself but also in relation to the way it is expressed. This suggests the possibility of an alternative approach that could link up with the notion of a specifically *artistic* sublime, broached provisionally earlier on in this essay. The crucial starting-point here is Kant's concept of 'genius', which is defined in § 46 as 'the innate mental aptitude . . . through which nature gives the rule to art'.[6]

Kant admits that this definition is stipulative, but holds that it is required in order to distinguish fine art from representations which merely communicate a subject-matter, or evoke pleasing sensations.

Now all art, as a mode of artifice, necessarily involves the following of rules pertaining to means and ends. Yet whereas in 'mechanical' and 'agreeable' art the artist's creativity is reducible to the following of established rules, in fine art it is not. Indeed

---

[6] Ibid. § 46, p. 168.

the very appearance of the fine art work has the unforced spontaneity of a natural object—thus belying its rule-governed origin in human artifice. In relation to the talent which the creation of such appearances presupposes, Kant observes that

such skill cannot be communicated, but requires to be bestowed directly from the hand of nature upon each individual, and so with him it dies, awaiting the day when nature once again endows another individual in the same way.[7]

Hence originality is the 'primary property' of genius. It should not, however, be thought that this is a sufficient condition. For, as Kant himself suggests, there can be 'original nonsense'.[8] What is required in addition is that the artist must have mastered the academic rules and conventions governing his medium. This not only allows him systematically to develop his gift of originality, but also enables the observer to judge that such originality is not just a passing fluke.

There are a number of issues which this theory raises. I shall concentrate on two. First, Kant has not really justified the stipulative character of his definition of genius. All that is required to distinguish fine art as a broad category from mechanical and agreeable art is that the former has an original element of handling which, while rule-governed, cannot be reduced to the following of rules. There is no need to invoke 'genius' (with its customary connotations of an *extraordinary* level of achievement) as a special term at all. Second, one cannot help but be uneasy at Kant's emphasis on the work of fine art having 'the appearance of nature'. This would suggest superficially that fine art's ultimate significance for us is as a free beauty—a source of pure aesthetic judgements. But Kant also insists that in judging the beauty of art 'the perfection of the thing must also be taken into account'[9] (i.e. we must judge it in relation to the end which defines things of that kind). This, though, would surely prevent us from experiencing it as a free beauty. We would have instead a putative case of that combination of the beautiful and the 'good' which, in § 16, Kant describes as dependent beauty. It is nevertheless interesting that Kant does not *explicitly* define fine art in such terms—and with good

---

[7] *Judgement*, § 47, p. 170.   [8] Ibid. § 46, p. 168.
[9] Ibid. § 48, p. 173.

reason. For if, as Kant holds, the end which defines fine art is the production of a beautiful appearance, then its beauty will have a logical bearing on its perfection, that is, will be cited as a reason (in fact *the* reason) for judging it to be a good instance of the kind of thing it is. This suggests that the relationship between beauty and reason in fine art is much more intimate than that 'combination' of the two which Kant describes in relation to dependent beauty. Indeed, I would suggest that it is the tacit recognition of this fact which leads Kant to a fundamental change of emphasis in his treatment of fine art in § 49. Specifically the product of genius is now linked to the notion of the 'aesthetic idea'. It is by considering some of the ramifications of this change of emphasis that we will further elaborate a specifically artistic sense of the sublime, and a less stipulative notion of genius.

First, then, Kant defines the aesthetic idea as

that representation of the imagination which induces much thought, yet without the possibility of any definite thought whatever, i.e. concept being adequate to it, and which language, consequently, can never get quite on level terms with or render completely intelligible.[10]

Kant then goes on to offer an important provisional analysis of why, in the aesthetic idea, concept is inadequate to intuition. The imagination, we are told, is able to 're-model experience' by following principles of reason, and, in so doing, produces an image that 'surpasses nature'. This special employment of imagination and the consequent surpassing of nature does not just consist in the fact that that artist can represent the supernatural (i.e. things which could never be encountered in the phenomenal world). For, as Kant points out in relation to the poet,

as to things of which examples occur in experience, e.g. death, envy, and all vices . . . transgressing the limits of experience he attempts with the aid of an imagination which emulates the display of reason in its attainment of a maximum, to body them forth to sense with a completeness of which nature affords no parallel.[11]

Clearly, if we are to explain in any depth why the aesthetic idea is more complete than nature, we must clarify the way in which it embodies the attainment of a maximum. This can be done (without invoking Kant's doctrine of the faculties) as follows. If an artist presents on the basis of his own experience, what *he* takes to be the most essential or interesting features of a subject-matter, and does so in an original style, then we will not simply assimilate that subject-matter in terms of its concept (i.e. just say 'here's a representation of an *x*'). Rather, because the subject-matter has been distended by the artist's style, our customary understanding of it, and the associations we form with it, will be challenged and transformed. This transformation can incline in three broad directions. First, we may attend to the strictly aesthetic aspect—the balance of phenomenal parts and whole in the artist's presentation of the subject-matter—and thus find that our capacity for conceptualizing is freely engaged. Second (a possibility which Kant does not consider), we may attend to the expressive aspect of the work, and identify with the artist, or with the particular emotions we find there, and their personal significance for us. In both these sorts of response, Kant's first (somewhat negative) definition of the aesthetic idea as a 'representation of the imagination which includes much thought' yet without any definite concept being adequate to it seems particularly appropriate. By transforming the world through the creation of an original image or sensuous configuration, the artist engages our cognitive and affective powers in a complex and deepened way.

This provides the clue for a second specifically artistic variety of sublimity. It may be that a work has such emotionally and/or imaginatively overwhelming *personal* significance for us that we are astonished at the fact that an artwork is able to 'hold' so much meaning. Here, in other words, the overwhelming personally significant associations serve to make vivid the scope of artistic creation. However, because the burden of meaning here falls on personal values, it seems unjustified to link this to genius. For even a bad work could—by dint of it having (for whatever reason) profound meaning in relation to one's own particular life—make the power of artistic creation vivid to us. I would suggest that if we are to make a more viable link between genius and artistic sublimity we must follow up a further clue provided by Kant. This consists in the fact that, as well as holding that the aesthetic idea is a representation of the imagination to which no concept is adequate, Kant also characterizes the aesthetic idea in a way that asserts a more positive relation between it and the concept which forms its starting-point. In this respect we are told that, if a representation of the imagination presents a concept in a way that induces much thought, then this gives

aesthetically an unbounded expansion to the concept itself . . . [Hence] it puts the faculty of intellectual ideas (reason) into motion—a motion, at the instance of a representation, towards an extension of thought, that, while germane, no doubt, to the concept of the object, exceeds what can be laid hold of in that representation or clearly expressed.[12]

We have here material for a harmony of reason and imagination which could have led Kant to a distinctively artistic notion of the sublime linked to genius. But he does not thus develop it. I shall attempt to do so in terms of a very liberal, but nevertheless plausible, reading of the above passage. Kant's basic point, I would suggest, can be construed as a claim to the effect that, if a concept is embodied in an aesthetic idea, this can lead the imagination to try and grasp a sense of the innumerable totality of instances which form the extension of that concept. The fact that the concept is schematized in such a vivid way leads us to try and schematize its many other ways of being instantiated. Our imagination, however, is soon overwhelmed by this, and we sense the immensity of those many instances from which the concept has been abstracted. Consider the statement 'old people are especially fallible'. This counts as a simple human truth in so far as it embodies the concept of a very familiar behavioural pattern. It also figures frequently as the subject-matter of, or as a theme in, works of art. With some artists this truth may be so acutely observed or rendered as to immerse us in associations pertaining to this particular instance of it. Yet in reading or seeing a performance of *King Lear*, the originality of Shakespeare's characterization and diction penetrates this particular instance of fallibility in old age so deeply and fully as to transcend particularity. We sense that Lear's situation is a tragic pattern of meaning which has been and will continue to be repeated in life at all times and places—indeed while ever it is possible for old people to hold positions of authority. We know, in other words, the truth which is Shakespeare's basic subject-matter, but the originality of his particular way of expressing it makes us

[12] *Judgement*, § 49, p. 177.

aware that Lear-type situations are infinitely repeatable; that is, it brings home that incomprehensible number of possible instantiations which make the subject-matter into a truth. The fact that this imaginatively overwhelming, as it were, *flesh* of the truth or concept is here evoked by a work of art serves to make vivid the extraordinary scope of artistic expression. While most artworks in some way please or engage us empathetically, or set up personal associations, there are a privileged few which do far more. They lead us to a sense that what makes a truth a truth is the fact that it can be realized universally (i.e. by occurring again and again in many different cultures and ages). Of course, there are mediocre artists who preach truth at us through their moralizing and political propaganda. But in such cases truth remains wholly abstract—it is something which we are simply *told*, and which we can grasp in purely linguistic terms. If, however, the artist can instantiate it in an image or sensible configuration of the profoundest style and originality, then here the truth is *realized*. This means that its universal applicability is sensuously evoked, and we are astounded by the fact that such an overwhelming possibility of meaning has been brought forth by human artifice. It is here, I would suggest, that we can talk with greatest justice of *sublime* art produced by *genius*.

I shall now move towards a conclusion with some cautionary comments which arise from Kant's account of aesthetic ideas in § 49. First, Kant has a tendency, when expressing himself in terms that point to a link between art and sublimity, to emphasize sublimity as a feature of content rather than sublimity of expression.[13] Yet the fact that I have used a work that happens to have a characteristically sublime content—blasted heaths, barbaric gougings, and the like—should not be taken as showing that sublimity of expression necessarily presupposes such a content. The fact that sublimity of expression does not presuppose intrinsically sublime subject-matter can be shown by the example (amongst others) of Van Gogh's famous painting of a pair of peasant boots. This is about as unsublime a subject-matter as one could hope for. However, as Heidegger has sensitively shown,[14] Van Gogh's sheer style of expression can open out a

[13] e.g. ibid. § 49, p. 178.
[14] In his 'The Origin of the Work of Art' included in *Heidegger: Basic Writings*, ed. D. F. Krell (Routledge & Kegan Paul: London, 1978), 163.

sense of the immense possibilities of toil and the passage of the seasons across the earth which inform the boots' truth as 'a piece of equipment'. A second worry about the points of emphasis in Kant's account of aesthetic ideas is his tendency to link the thrusting of the mind 'beyond its own ken' to those special significatory devices which he labels 'attributes'.[15] I would suggest, though, that sublimity of expression has no intrinsic link with any specific signifying device. A *Fête galante* by Watteau, for instance, can convey (against a backcloth of Arcadian generality) an astonishing sense of the infinite repeatability of what (for the person experiencing them) are essentially transient moments of love. Yet we in no way have to regard it as an allegory of time. Indeed, the tendency to use overt symbolism, metaphor, and the like can meet with the same fate as the conventionalized 'sublime' content of the Gothic novel and late eighteenth-century landscape painting (i.e. degenerate into clichéd theatricality). There are so many works *heavy* with Christian symbolism that it is only when a familiar symbolic device is played off against one of striking singularity (as, for example, St Peter's gesture of benediction against the beardless 'pagan' Christ in Botticelli's *Pietà*) that we sense the enormity of the tragedy and redemptive possibilities that are figured in Christ's death.

I have, by developing themes in Kant's theory of art, shown that, despite his reservations, the sublime can arise in a threefold distinctively artistic sense. Either through the overwhelming perceptual scale of a work making vivid the scope of human artifice, or through a work's overwhelming personal significance making vivid the scope of artistic creation, or, finally, through the imaginatively overwhelming character of some general truth embodied in a work, making vivid the scope of artistic expression. Of course, it is true that (as in the case of sublimity which arises when the scope of rational cognition is made vivid by sheer size or intensity in nature) sublimity in its artistic modes cannot be indifferent to the 'real existence' of its object. We would not find *King Lear* sublime if we knew that it had, in fact, been written by a monkey with a strange fluency in the handling of quill pens. However, it can count as *relatively* disinterested in so far as to enjoy a work's sublimity does not presuppose that we

---

[15] *Judgement*, § 49, p. 177.

take it to be of direct utility in relation to the network of our practical or theoretical needs, aims, and interests. Our enjoyment of the sublimity of art is, rather, *for its own sake*, and involves a felt compatibility between the sensible world and human creative capacities, inasmuch as it is a sensible item which is here vivifying our creative capabilities. We are thereby made 'at home' with the world as both sensible and rational beings.

I have, then, reconstructed Kant's theory of the sublime in terms of four varieties. The first of these (which I shall call the *cognitive* variety) divides into the mathematical and dynamical modes; it arises when some vast or powerful object (whether real or occurring as the subject-matter in art) makes vivid the scope of rational cognition as such. The second variety—which I shall call the *artefactual* sublime—arises when some vast or mighty man-made product (or a representation of one) makes vivid the scope of human artifice. The third variety—which I shall call the *personalized* sublime—involves some overwhelming personal significance that an artwork holds for us making vivid the scope of artistic creation. The final variety—which I shall term the *expressive* sublime—arises when an artist's originality is able to evoke a sense of his subject-matter's universal significance and, in so doing, makes vivid the extraordinary scope of artistic expression. All these varieties (as I noted above) are relatively disinterested modes of appreciation, and each of them involves an element of felt compatibility between the sensible world and some specific human capacity. These considerations, I would suggest, establish the sublime as a distinctive aesthetic concept. They also square with ordinary usage (which I mentioned in the Introduction to this study) in so far as the cognitive and artefactual varieties parallel our *descriptive* use of the term sublime, and the personalized and expressive varieties parallel its *evaluative* sense. It may be that the sublime has been, and will continue to be, used in a very broad fashion, but the four kindred experiences I have described form its logical core. Indeed they enable us formally to offer a general definition: the sublime is an item or set of items which, through the possession or suggestion of perceptually, imaginatively, or emotionally overwhelming properties, succeeds in rendering the scope of some human capacity vivid to the senses. This definition also provides the means to an important reinterpretation of the history of aesthetic sensibility. To show this would involve a major study in itself. However, I shall at least sketch an outline of how such an investigation might proceed.

II

The basis of my reappraisal of sublimity's relevance to the history of sensibility will derive fundamentally from the cognitive and artefactual varieties. A first point to note is that, in a sense, Kant did his job too well. For him, the experience of sublimity focuses on nature, and the arguments of the third *Critique* provide a massive and influential legitimization of this emphasis. The idea of nature as the major object of aesthetic sensibility is a view closely associated with the rise of Romanticism in the late eighteenth and early nineteenth centuries. I would suggest, therefore, that Kant's emphatic linking of the sublime to nature has left it profoundly associated with the Romantic era. This is why it has struck so many as being an 'outmoded' concept. But, as my reconstruction has shown, the sublime can also encompass the domain of human artifice and contrivance. This places the history of the sublime in a somewhat different perspective.

To show this I shall consider a passage from Zola's novel *Germinal*. Here the coal mine manager has just told the representatives of striking miners that if they have no confidence in him, they should take their demands 'down there' . . .

Where was 'down there'? Paris presumably. But they could not say for sure; the whole question was receding into some distant and terrifying place, some far off, metaphysical region where the unknown god was crouching on his throne in the depths of the tabernacle. They would never see this god, but they felt him as a power, weighing down from afar on the ten thousand miners of Montsou. And when the manager spoke, he had this hidden power behind him and pronounced its oracles.[16]

The 'hidden power' referred to here is, of course, Capital. In the late nineteenth century the experience of society becomes fundamentally an urban one organized around the capitalist

[16] Emile Zola, *Germinal*, trans. L. W. Tancock (Penguin: Harmondsworth, 1968), 217.

economy. This organization implies at once order and disorder. Order, in so far as capitalism is a force for cohesion; disorder in so far as it involves crisis, and oppression, and breeds revolt. In the society which grows around this structure of order/disorder, we can see a displacement of the sublime from nature to the urban experience. In this experience there is a fascination with Capital as a mighty power or god (as the passage from Zola shows) and with the direct products of Capital; yet at the same time there is an equal fascination with its epiphenomena and with patterns of resistance to it. Vast urban landscapes, violent mobs and crowds, the prospect of revolutionary violence. But why is there a fascination with things of this sort? To some degree one can explain it in terms of the psychology of human interests. Some people are fascinated by Capital and its products because they take their own material well-being to be bound up with the system's smooth operations; while others are fascinated precisely because Capital is a monster which must be studied in order to make its destruction the easier. However, there comes a point where Capital and the forces it generates are enjoyed *for their own sake* as an aesthetic spectacle. Zola's worker-hero Étienne Lantier often regards the 'hidden monster' with awe rather than hatred, and one suspects that this is true of Zola himself. Similar considerations arise in relation to the images and sentiments used in and *aroused by* the political writings of Marx, Bakunin, and others. We are given a sense of mighty forces set in motion and combat with one another—revolutionary 'spectres' haunt 'the citadels of power', etc. These battles are fought around conflicting visions of human interest, but I would suggest that the vision of conflict itself—the theory and practice of revolutionary violence in relation to the capitalist system—marks the new context wherein the experience of sublimity is displaced from its previous orientation towards nature.

The fact that this displacement remains unrecognized for so long is due to the fact that, when it is experienced in the context of political conflicts and societal structures, it is difficult to separate aesthetic responses from those bound up with practical issues. Now the *rhetoric* of sublime imagery has always had a place in the theory and practice of politics. But my point is that in the age of capitalist power and mass politics this assumes a new importance and is given a concrete directness. The structures of capitalism and the conflicts it engenders provide immediate and inescapable images that overwhelm our perceptual or imaginative powers, yet make the scope of rational comprehension or human artifice and contrivance all the more vivid. The spectacle fascinates us in itself, and irrespective of its broader practical significance for us.

This displacement of the sublime has carried over into the twentieth century albeit with a change of emphasis. The burden of the aesthetic spectacle has shifted somewhat from revolutionary politics to the products and epiphenomena bound up with technological innovation in the capitalist and state capitalist systems. Military parades and mechanized warfare exert renewed fascination, the image of the twentieth-century city as a vast anonymous domain of mysterious and violent multitudes figures large in the subject-matter of literature, painting, and the cinema. Images of space travel and science fiction likewise enjoy enormous popularity. In all these examples we find a fascination with vastness and power that transcends any immediate practical relevance for us. We experience the sublime.

I do appreciate that the foregoing outline is somewhat speculative in character and goes beyond the purview of strictly philosophical analysis. It counts rather as the beginnings of a *genealogy* of the sublime in the postmodern era; that is, a study which will consider the shifting societal and intellectual conditions which have enabled sublimity to figure once more in the forefront of cultural discourse. It is to be hoped, therefore, that, as well as clarifying Kant's theory, the present study will also provide the basis of an adequate philosophical framework for the construction of such a genealogy.

III

To bring this book to a fitting conclusion, it is now worth briefly addressing a question that is much in keeping with Kant's fundamental strategy in the third *Critique* as a whole. The question is—what broader metaphysical and moral significance does the sublime have for us? In this respect, we will recall that for Kant our pleasure in the sublime is due to the triumph of our rational over our sensible being—a triumph that is eminently concordant with the demands of morality. I argued, however, that Kant links sublimity and morality rather too closely. In effect, he reduces the sublime to a kind of indirect moral experience. As an alternative to this I proposed that we should regard the sublime as an experience wherein some perceptually, imaginatively, or emotionally overwhelming aspect of the sensible world serves to make the scope of specific human capacities vivid to the senses. The ground of our pleasure here consists, in other words, of a felt harmony between the sensible world and our cognitive capacities or creative abilities.

In order to have experiences of this sort, it is not necessary that we are explicitly aware of what, philosophically speaking, such experiences involve. True, our judgements must be informed at *some* level of consciousness by knowledge as to our sensible limitations and the scope of our rational and creative capacities, but this knowledge need not figure overtly. Indeed, the experience is of such complexity and of such characteristic affective power that we will rarely be able to offer adequate reasons for our response. Let us suppose, though, that we accept the theory of sublimity which I have proposed, and that knowledge of this theory now informs our experiences of the sublime. In such a case, it could be claimed that an essentially aesthetic experience now points towards important metaphysical and moral insights. One might argue as follows. The capacity for rational comprehension is a fundamental feature of our everyday existence. For example, we recognize that physical objects form phenomenal wholes even if all the parts which go to make up such wholes are not immediately accessible to the senses. In our theoretical or practical projects, we can calculate or comprehend even the vastest and most powerful items in terms of rational concepts. This capacity to comprehend phenomena which far exceed our immediate perceptual and physical grasp is the major feature which sets humanity aside from other members of the animal world. Yet the very fact that the capacity is so intrinsic to our being, and is so extensively employed, tends to desensitize our awareness of it. It is taken for granted as a kind of useful tool with which we control and manipulate reality. Philosophy can draw our attention to reason, but even here our understanding of it is characteristically reified. It is known as a 'property' or 'quality' 'accruing' to human beings, rather than as a dynamic and extraordinary mode of transcendence towards the world. Similar considerations held in relation to another crucial element in the sublime, namely our awareness of perceptual and bodily limitations—in short, our sense of finitude. When this sense presses upon us in everyday life it is, characteristically, as a nuisance or hindrance to our projects. More powerful but perhaps even more negative intimations of it are forced upon us when we witness suffering, illness, and death. Philosophers—especially the existential sort—have stressed that a radical sense of finitude is a pre-condition of 'authentic' existence (i.e. of being fully aware of one's freedom, and of our distinctively human mode of being in the world). But this fact—this positive dimension of finitude—is rather hard to keep in view, and especially so in those distressing situations when our sense of finitude is felt most acutely. I am suggesting, then, that in everyday life, and even in philosophical discourse, the full existential force and poignancy of being rational and finite tends to be submerged or distorted. In the context of the sublime, however, a rather different experience of what it is to be a finite rational being emerges. What is important here is not simply the fact that the sublime vivifies the extraordinary scope of rational comprehension (in a way that pierces through our normal desensitization); but also the fact that it is experienced as profoundly and inseparably connected with—indeed, as *called forth and projected from*—finite being's struggle to launch itself into and articulate the world. In this experience, in other words, both rationality and finitude are experienced as a kind of positive and integrated continuity. They are felt to embody a fundamental thrust where the primal drama of the very origin and essence of the human condition itself is re-enacted and exemplified.

The approach which I have just taken in relation to the cognitive sublime can also be applied to the artefactual and expressive varieties. We use artefacts and take them for granted, almost as if they were products of nature which happen to be conveniently placed for our use. Again with expressive artefacts—such as pulp literature or TV soap operas—our fundamental encounter with them is in consumerist terms; that is, with regard to their pleasurable escapist effects rather than to their causal origins in human skill and creativity. Of course, some utilitarian and expressive artefacts do engage us in terms other than these. We may take pleasure in well-made or ornate furniture, or enjoy an aesthetic empathy with the particular vision of the world embodied in some artwork. But to experience such artefacts as sublime involves their perceptually, imaginatively, or emotionally overwhelming properties, making vivid the scope of human artifice or expression itself. This means, in effect, that we are again returned to the very origins and essence of such capacities—namely their existence as aspects of a distinctively human *mode of being* called forth by finitude's struggle to contain and direct the demands of the sensible and/or social world. All artifice and expression has its source in this primal urge to transcendence. But it is the sublime work which best evokes and exemplifies such a drama of origins.

There is a further dimension of metaphysical significance related to the above, but which focuses specifically on the mathematical sublime (i.e. those occasions when some vast or hugely complex item of sensibility vivifies the scope of rational comprehension). Again, the unearthing of this significance takes as its premiss features which are concealed or distorted in everyday life. The features in question here are spatiality and temporality. Our everyday experiences of these are structured by our practical projects. For example, we travel from location *a* to location *b*; the spaces we inhabit are known as places of work, or leisure, or domicile. Likewise we divide up time in terms of things to be done, deadlines to be met, hours for work, and hours for leisure, etc. In the realm of more theoretical projects (such as certain aspects of physics) spatiality and temporality are known more overtly—but only as those mathematically articulated constructs which we call 'space' and 'time'. Here our experience is not of *lived* spatiality and temporality, but of abstractions *from* these. I am suggesting, in other words, that there is a more primordial experience of spatiality and temporality which our everyday practical or theoretical projects articulate, but at the same time conceal or distort. To recover this primordial experience we must understand spatiality and temporality as a unified fundamental horizon of human existence. This means that our sense of spatial presence and the present moment must first be explicitly informed by a sense of presences and presents which have passed beyond our immediate grasp or recall, and by an anticipation of the unknown number of future presences and presents still to be experienced. This constitutes the threshold of our recuperative task.

Before advancing to the second and decisive stage, we must follow up a clue provided by Kant. In § 27 of the Critique of Aesthetic Judgement, we are told the following:

Measurement of a space (as apprehension) is at the same time a description of it, and so an objective movement in the imagination and a progression. On the other hand the comprehension of the manifold in the unity, not of thought, but of intuition, and consequently the comprehension of the successively apprehended parts at one glance, is a retrogression that removes the time-condition in the progression of the imagination, and renders *co-existence* intuitable. Therefore, since the time-series is a condition of the internal sense and of an intuition, it is a subjective movement of the imagination by which it does violence to the internal sense—a violence which must be proportionately more striking the greater the quantum which the imagination comprehends in one intuition.[17]

Kant's basic point here is that our customary experience of sensible items is founded on temporally successive apprehension of parts in the manifold of intuition. However, by an act of 'violence' to time we can suspend this progression and grasp all the parts in a single intuition of the whole. This means that, given some phenomenal whole or totality, we can perceptually or imaginatively grasp it *as* a whole or totality, without having successively to discriminate all its parts. The main point of interest here, though, lies in one claim which Kant makes explicitly, and one which is left implicit. The explicit point is the one concerning how the act of 'violence' becomes more striking in proportion to the greatness of the manifold we are trying to comprehend. Suppose that we encounter some vast object, and strive to comprehend it in terms of some perceptual viewpoint or image which will fully express its size in relation to our physical frame. This can, indeed, be done 'at a glance'. Seeing a mountain in the distance, for example, we recognize immediately that it dwarfs the human frame into utter insignificance. Yet there are those dramatic occasions when we make some attempt to comprehend this relation in rather more complete perceptual or imaginative terms. We may do it by trying to imagine all the effort and time it would take to climb or traverse the mountain, or by imagining the innumerable different views or aspects that would be revealed in our exploration. Here, it is as though there is some power within us which drives us fully to comprehend the object's size in relation to us, in terms of some single perception or image or contained set of perceptions or image-sequences. In cases such as these, where we strive for total imaginative comprehension, our engagement with spatio-temporality is at its most violent. For here we are trying to compress a hugely extendable sequence of successively apprehended parts or aspects of the object into a single contained phenomenal whole. In a by now familiar quotation from § 26 of the Critique of Aesthetic Judgement, Kant shows just what is involved in such an exercise. We are told that

if the apprehension has reached a point beyond which the representations of sensuous intuition in the case of the parts first apprehended begin to disappear from the imagination as this advances to the apprehension of yet others, as much, then, is lost at one end as is gained at the other, and for comprehension we get a maximum which the imagination cannot exceed.[18]

On these terms the attempt at total perceptual or imaginative comprehension of a vast object's size in relation to us involves a violent struggle. We are strikingly aware of the object's presence in our present, but this is because our experience of it is felt, as it were, to be fraying at both edges. For even as the many views or images and the moments of their experience slip beyond immediate awareness into the past, we also feel a striking anticipation of many views and moments of experience yet to come. Our perceptual and imaginative capacities are swamped. We are thus on the threshold of a primordial experience of spatio-temporality. Yet this is only a threshold. For left here, we would experience this horizon only in terms of a kind of existential vertigo or nausea, wherein we felt ourselves to be of, yet overwhelmed by, the spatio-temporal. Our experience would remain incomplete and negative. But what if, under such circumstances, we experience the object as *sublime*, rather than simply overwhelming? What extra dimension is involved here? It

---

[18] *Judgement*, § 27, p. 99.

is at this juncture that we must advert back to the point which Kant left implicit in the quotation before last. For while it is a 'subjective movement of the imagination' which does violence to time in our comprehension of phenomenal wholes, it is (as I showed in Chapter 4) the faculty of *reason* which instigates this.

Now, putting all this in terms of my revised version of Kant's theory, one might argue as follows. Our capacity for rational comprehension (in the most general sense) guides and directs the flow of phenomenal experience by enabling us to grasp wholes and totalities, without always having successively to apprehend their parts. It enables us to cope with reality by abbreviating the spatio-temporal complexity of the phenomenal world. In the experience of vast objects, however—even though we may know it to be an impossible task at the outset—we sometimes attempt to grasp the object's phenomenal totality in terms of some synoptic set of perceptions or images which fully express the object's immensity in relation to us. The fact that this cannot be done will either fill us with existential vertigo, or lead us to find the object sublime. The reason why this latter response is possible is because the violent failure of our perceptual or imaginative capacities can make the power of our capacity for rational comprehension all the more vivid. On the one hand we sense its *directive force* (i.e. the way it is able to organize our perceptual and imaginative engagement with the world, and even push this beyond its limits); on the other hand, we have an enhanced feeling of the *scope* of rational comprehension, in so far as we know that the object forms a limited whole in time and space, and that (no matter how overwhelming the task might be in perceptual or imaginative terms) we can in principle *fully* comprehend its size in relation to us through the use, say, of mathematical concepts. Given this, one might say that to experience the sublime in these terms is to have a full and complete primordial experience of spatio-temporality. This is not only because a sublime experience of this sort involves a heightened awareness of past and future presences and moments as flowing out from our present awareness of some overwhelming spatial object, but also because the felt violence of this encounter enhances our awareness of the fact that *qua* rational beings we can direct and, to some degree, even circumscribe the flow. We experience ourselves as simultaneously immanent and transcendent in terms of the spatio-temporal flux. We sense ourselves to be, as it were, *of* it, *in* it, and *astride* it. It is this primordial structure of spatio-temporal immanence and transcendence which is shaped but concealed by the everyday world of our practical and theoretical projects.

I am arguing, then, that our various experiences of the sublime can have a broader *metaphysical* significance in terms of what might be called 'primordial disclosure'. By this, I mean that the sublime is an affective experience which *qua* aesthetic is logically distinguishable from those connected with the immediate vicissitudes of everyday life, but which, if understood correctly, reveals a foundation in ultimate structures which are immanent to, but customarily concealed within, that life. This is not simply a case of aesthetic experience acting as a kind of affective exclamation mark to be placed after some philosophical insight. Rather what the aesthetic experience hinges upon here— namely the projection of rational comprehension from a finite base—is itself a dramatic exemplar of several fundamental relationships which philosophy tries to recover and express. If, therefore, we enjoy such an experience and at the same time know what is involved in it, we have a more primordial way of understanding some of our fundamental relations to the world than that which is afforded by purely philosophical knowledge. In primordial disclosure, in other words, reflective knowledge dwells close to the points of its own origin.

Let me now consider (albeit very briefly) how our understanding of the sublime might also point generally in the direction of moral insight. First, in our own culture what counts as morality is a topic of controversy. However, almost all protagonists in the debate would admit that, whatever else it involves, morality entails *respect for persons*, that is the belief that the individual human has a *worth* of a wholly different order to that which we would place upon inanimate objects or, indeed, other members of the animal kingdom. There are many reasons which might be given in justification of such a view, but most of them relate to the fact that our capacity for rational comprehension is something which gives human experience a depth and intensity that is without match in the known universe. Let us suppose that we experience the cognitive sublime and have an understanding of what the experience involves. This means that our sense of

what is most distinctive and extraordinary about human beings—
our projection of rational comprehension through the vicissitudes
of sensible embodiment—is given a powerful affective exemplification. We may know that all human beings have the potential to
comprehend things which far exceed their sensible capacities, but
to countenance this fact through an experience of the sublime is
to experience it, as it were, *from the inside*. This might be
interpreted as a secular exemplar of the old adage that every
human being possesses a spark of the divine. Given that through
experiences of the cognitive sublime we can become vividly aware
of the utter extraordinariness of what it is to be human, then we
might reasonably hope that such experiences will be conducive to
our sense of respect for persons.

In the case of the artefactual and the expressive sublime,
slightly different considerations hold. Here what is made vivid by
the overwhelming object is the scope of human artifice or
expression, as such. If such experiences are informed by a
knowledge of what is involved in them, then they can again
dramatically exemplify the extraordinary capacities and achieve-
ments of humanity, and thence lead us to identify with our
species' conquest of overwhelming or intractable nature. Given,
therefore, this striking and enhanced enjoyment of *species
solidarity*, one again has reasonable grounds for hoping that the
sublime will be conducive to our sense of respect for persons.

In conclusion, it must be stressed that the broader metaphysical
and moral significance which I have assigned to the sublime
is not a dimension which figures in it explicitly *qua* aesthetic
experience. At the aesthetic level, rather, our pleasure is
grounded solely in the felt harmony between the sensible world
and some rational or creative capacity in ourselves. It is this
harmony, indeed, which makes the aesthetic a logically distinct
kind of experience. But if our experience is also informed by an
understanding of the elements involved in it, *then* it can engender
the kind of metaphysical and moral insights which I have
described. The approach I have taken in this respect again takes
us considerably beyond Kant's own theory. The distance
involved here, however, is not quite as great as it might at first
seem. For while we rightly think of Kant as striving to establish
the distinctive grounds of aesthetic experience, his overall
strategy in the third *Critique* aims at considerably more.

Specifically, he wishes to show that the aesthetic experience's metaphysical *raison d'être* is, in the final analysis, to promote our existence as moral beings. Kant's arguments for this are (as I have shown earlier) deeply unsatisfactory. Yet they do contain one insight of capital importance—namely the very fact that, while logically distinct, *aesthetic experience does not exist in a vacuum*. It has important connections with broader aspects of human existence. In this final section I have attempted to follow this clue by showing how the sublime can lead to metaphysical and moral insights. Again, in other words, we go beyond what Kant himself would have ascribed to, but the insight which guides us is ultimately his. He saw (however opaquely) that aesthetic experience—and the sublime in particular—has the capacity to *humanize*.

INDEX